Church Girl, Club Girl, ~~~ ~ ~...

Copyright © Brandi L. Rojas

ISBN: 978-1-7373229-5-5

LOC: Confirmed and Accepted

Publisher, Editor and Book Design:

Fiery Beacon Publishing House, LLC

Fiery Beacon Consulting and Publishing Group

Graphics: FBPH Graphics Team, Dashona Smith

CHURCH GIRL,

CLUB GIRL,

GOD'S GIRL.

Brandi L. Rojas

DEDICATION

To my Husband, Apostle Omar Rojas, thank you for loving me and supporting my truth in hopes of freeing someone else.

To my children, may my vulnerability always serve as a point of reference to what I have already defeated on your behalf. May every giant I slay in His name, be added to your credit and remain powerless to defeat you, too.

To every person that didn't know what else to call it outside of church hurt, this is for you.

TABLE OF CONTENTS

I. THE CHURCH

II. THE CLUB

III. GOD

THE
CHURCH

1.

ALTARS AND ALTERS

January 17, 2022 was the day that these chapter titles were officially downloaded in my spirit, just when I thought that I had it all perfected. This day, otherwise known as MLK Day, is often noted as a day of freedom and equality, but to be honest, my life has never felt quite "free" or "equal." If you will allow me this space and time, I would be honored to explain.

I really don't believe that I have never "not" been in church. Even as a child, I was always drawn to it. I remember being seven years old and telling my mother that the next Sunday the opportunity was presented, I was going to go to the altar to give my life to Christ. Though I cannot remember my mother's response, I do remember being able to freely walk up when the day and the moment came. I remember being excited, regardless of the fact that I was on the verge of making one of the biggest decisions of my life not to mention the army that I had just enlisted myself in. As with most congregations, there is something about the moment that a child comes up to the altar; the church seems to always go into an uproar while most will only offer a few claps for an adult that finally gives God a YES. In that moment, none of that mattered to me. I wanted to give my life to this God who had an innate ability to make people shout, yell, scream, smile through tears, fall out and more. Yes, I wanted HIM.

In the years following, I guess I became one of the poster kids of the ministry. Once the youth ministry was established, it felt as though I had been picked out of the litter, but not before losing my father. You see, at fourteen, not only did my Daddy pass away, but I found myself days later, commemorating his life at the very altar that I had given my life to Christ at just seven years before. I have to say, I was in so much shock that I didn't have an equal moment to even be mad at God. I remember the day after his passing, my mother felt that it would be a good idea for me to go to school, you know, to keep the normalcy of things while she made plans. My mother was so noble during that time in our lives, because despite their divorce several years before, she would still check on him, make him sweet potato pies and yes, at that moment, even help to finalize his arrangements while still calling him "Husband;" In fact, that was the first time in my life that I can remember her actually calling him "her husband."

That time in my life was so pivotal. It was after this tragedy that my youth pastor at the time saw something in me, and without hesitation, began to cultivate and push me into those directions. As so many churches do, we had something called Youth Sunday – this was the time when the youth led the service for the day, or at least made their presence very much known. For some reason, my youth pastor felt that God had a Word He wanted to speak through me and asked me to do just that. I had never spoken on a platform like that; in fact, the closest I had ever gotten was through me singing in the choir. The preparation I remember vividly as my mother took me to the Christian book store to find just the right book to assist me in this new assignment that had been placed on my life which I accepted nervously, and yet, with no rejection.

The day finally came, and though I cannot remember how I felt or even the title of my "speech", I remember having my words written out and ready to read. I mounted the platform, and I promise you, it felt as if the whole room got completely silent. I began to read what I had written, as I tried to ensure my clarity and flow. Before I knew it, I saw my Senior Pastor at that time stand on his feet, followed by the infamous move that he would always make when someone was doing their "good preaching," as he rubbed his forehead. Before I knew it, other people in the sanctuary stood up on their feet too, but I knew I had to finish, so I just kept reading. I do not recall how I stepped away from the microphone or anything else about that moment, but I do remember just being glad that it was over, as I stood in the space where I pursued God at seven and now, sharing the first Word that God had given me at fourteen.

In the Old Testament, altars had a totally different approach and usage in comparison to now. Back then, animals were slaughtered as a sacrifice to get God's attention. Places were reserved for priests only, as they traveled from the outer courts to the inner courts and the holies of holies. Those places were deemed so sacred, that they would even put a bell around the priest's ankle before he entered, so if he stopped moving or stayed in longer than recommended, they could ring the bell to find out if he was not just conscious, but if he was even alive. Yea, the presence of God was that heavy. These altars over time, have become a place of dedication, rededication, sacrifice and the infamous YES. It has been filled with promise after promise, so much so that people become irritated at the sign of a person who goes to the altar for the 1,000[th] time hoping that God will grant them another stint of grace. Sadly, the ones who are often irritated should probably be up there too, as God in those moments reveals the impatience of their hearts when He has been ever so patient with them.

As I look back now, the one thing that I can say I never received "the talk" about, was the things that I would face as a result of my decision. As a seven-year-old, some probably felt that I was too young to make the decision, but I didn't care about the consequence at that moment, I just wanted what I had decided on and had waited for days to accept. Though I was young, that was not my only time coming to the altar, and most definitely was not the only YES that I gave to God, but regardless, the conversation I probably needed never happened.

This walk won't be a bed of roses.

Everything won't be perfect just because you told God YES.

You will still have trials and tribulations, and maybe even more with this bullseye on your back now.

Ok, I know that this doesn't sound very "disciple-ish" or even evangelistic in nature, but in all seriousness, I wish someone had at least prepared me for what I would endure. You see, in our culture, the method of raising children has been with the understanding that they are not privy to the trials and situations that adults go through — that is known as "grown folks' business." I can only imagine how many generations have gone through unnecessarily because they simply didn't know. Their experiences soon became a question of what they did wrong, not what the generation before them decided not to kill before they got here. Before we know it, we find ourselves carrying the sins and cycles of our bloodline simply because we were never told that we could instead, kill them. Truthfully, it makes sense, for how can someone else tell you that you need to kill it when they never even tried to load the gun clip?

As an editor, it used to make me chuckle to see people spell ALTAR as ALTER; though that was their mistake, God uses everything, right? It is often at the altar, that God gives us the opportunity to be altered. It is here that our dingy whites are made pearly white and our slate is made clean. It is here that though the world outside the doors has not changed, we are granted another chance with an eternal God who is more than willing to forgive forget as we repent to Him as He alters our current garments for redemptive ones.

[4] He spoke to those who stood before Him, saying, "Remove the filthy garments from him." And He said to Joshua, "See, I have caused your wickedness to be taken away from you, and I will clothe *and* beautify you with rich robes [of forgiveness]."

Zechariah 3:4

One of the major lessons that we learn about this altar and the alteration, is that though God forgives as He does, man does not operate under the same law or processes. In our world, we say it this way: "I will forgive you but I will never forget." It is here that in the same breath, we will ask God to forgive us, to ALTER us, while we hold on to the offense concerning others for sake of our own protection. Personally, I have been known to forgive and forgive quickly and let people right back in, at least before wisdom kicked in (you will have to make it to the end of the book to get that story.) Seriously, someone could do the worst, but I would forgive almost immediately, because in my mind, I just wanted everything to be okay like it was before according to my judgement. It was through my teenage years that I realized that was unheard of. I remember taking a dance class once at our elective school here in the city. I cannot remember the circumstances, but I recall two girls, sisters, one of which could not stand me. For me, not being liked was not anything new; since I was one of the only tenth graders at my school with a car, that automatically made me a target. We walked down the hall to prepare for class, and as we did, all I could hear was this girl walking behind me saying what she was going to do to me, nevertheless I kept walking. We finally made it in the dressing room as she immediately stepped to me while her sister and other friends surrounded us.

I can't stand you b** **! I'm gonna beat you're a**!

I stood there, nervous as all outdoors. Before I knew it, I opened my mouth and said,

It's ok. I love you and God does, too.

Wait! What? Here stood this girl ready to take me out and the only response I had was the love of Jesus?

She looked, her eyes became even more red as she said through gritting teeth....

I don't give a d*** about you or your God. I'm gonna beat your a**!

Despite her threat my response remained the same until finally, by some act I cannot remember, the altercation was broken up. Believe it or not, after that day she never messed with me again.

As it was with this incident, it proceeded to be that way with life as the years progressed. Regardless of what I went through until high school graduation, I never let go of God. In fact, I was often spotted playing Kirk Franklin and other gospel artists at max volume through the system I had installed in my car! Most of my friends were white, even down to my "play sister", Crystal, who had gladly adopted the title of "my twin." So there I was, from Phillips Avenue, Woodmere Park and the only black girl in the tenth grade with a car and primarily white friends. Needless to say, this became problematic as I would often return to my car after school to find it keyed to the high heavens. While some of my childhood friends had decided to become part of a "local gang" and make me one of their targets, what they did not realize was that I did not get my car because I was rich, bougee or any of the sort, but instead, because of the passing of my father and the provision left behind.

Now before you assume that my childhood was horrendous, let me combat that with this — it was having a car that introduced me to my best friend and high school who is now my sister for life, Tyresha. She was bold, fearless, and because she was from Phoenix, no one dared to mess with her. She and her sister, Sharesha was known for even taking some of the football team out — they were NO JOKE! To this day, I cannot confirm how we even became friends, but I know that by senior year we were inseparable. Senior year also became the year that I made a life-changing, life-altering move, leaving my childhood church for a new one.

This opportunity did not come by normal means but instead by the offer of someone who we will call, Melissa. She was spunky, fun, made me laugh, was older than me and was a co-worker of mine. One day she somehow convinced me that it was okay to do something that could have been detrimental to my job and boy did I pay the price. When I say price, I mean to the point where she said it was all me and had NOTHING to do with her, but not before inviting me to go to church with her (Fix your face, it gets better.) When she invited me, it seemed like the perfect idea, since I was feeling a pull to shift into liturgical dance, which at that point in time was viewed as out of order and more within the church universal and the church I was currently attending. She assured me that I would love it — that there were people there my age and that the church was extremely progressive.

Sunday morning came, and to be honest, my biggest issue was not what to wear but what to tell my mom. I knew that her expectation was that we would go to church together, but this day, I decided that I wanted to visit this "new and progressive ministry." She didn't put up much fuss, which made me feel at ease, but little did I know what I was about to walk into. You see, my church had hundreds, but this one looked as if it had millions who were welcoming, friendly and most of all, loud! There I was, seventeen years old, walking in a church where I "thought" I knew no one. When I first arrived, Melissa greeted me with a huge, welcoming grin. I smiled back and sped over to where she was. The doors opened and all I could do was look around like a deer in headlights. People were excited, hype even and ready to worship God. I saw teens my age on fire, and even serving. I took my seat ready for the next moment, which would eventually lead to the next thirteen years of my life. It was here that I learned about God in a whole, new and undeniable way. It was here that I learned about taking "real notes in church," some of which I still have to this day. It was here that I learned about Holy Spirit and soon went from just hearing about Him to accepting Him along with the gift of speaking as the Spirit of God gave utterance. It was also here that I committed to a relationship that would soon try to destroy my soul.

As people, I believe that we all have that moment where we decide that we will not fall victim to the tragedies we see; for me, those things included abuse, and yes, teen pregnancy, too. Between church, work and school, senior year was moving like lightning and beyond getting ready for college and the prom, the Beautillion was a really big deal. At that time, I was part of a youth organization in the city and had become friends with a guy name Chad. Now this guy was tall, sweet and found himself asking me to escort him for this fraternal event to which I gladly accepted. The weekend for the event finally came and it was there that I met this guy who had the most amazing sense of humor, and who made my heart melt on sight; let's call him Brandon. I don't know, maybe it was the way he made me laugh or the concern he seemingly displayed, but the cherry on the top for me, was finding out that he was "in church," and not only that but a Minister-in-Training.

Within weeks we went from being complete strangers, to dating. I had visited his church and everyone for the most part knew that we were together. Everything about him seemed perfect, and those moments erased every red flag that I should have seen. When he would minister, I would be right there front and center, ready for the Word to pour out of him. I was captivated by the fire he displayed, as he perfectly mimicked every preacher he looked up to, while grabbing their "oil" and claiming it as his own. It didn't take long before he began demanding that he become the primary voice in my life, get rid of my friends, and stay away from any other guys regardless of our relationship. Being a daddy's girl, I craved affirmation and protection, and that desire trumped the isolation he had mandated in my life; as sick as it sounds to say now, I saw his demands as being the covering I needed, and fully accepted it.

I will never forget the day that he accused me of cheating on him. It was a perfect day when he called and demanded that I come to his house. I dropped everything I was doing at that moment, gave my mother some excuse to leave, jumped in my car and rushed over. When he opened the door, he had a look I had never seen before, one of rage and pure hatred. He didn't even say hello, but instead opened the door and walked away from me. "Hey," I said with suspicion; he didn't say a word but instead, walked away and went in the kitchen. I came behind him trying to embrace him, but he waved me away and continued to walk. There I stood, clueless in the living room waiting for his return. He came back in with a juice glass filled with water, took a sip, and then hurled it at my head. To this day I know it had to be God who protected me, because he threw it straight at my head, but instead it curved and ran into the fireplace.

I didn't have words.

I couldn't even breathe.

He approached me full speed ahead, yelling and throwing insults. He told me that he knew I had cheated on him, and the louder he got as he accused me was met with my insisting that I hadn't done a thing. He told me that I had embarrassed and insulted him and he knew what I had done. I soon found myself begging,

"You're scaring me! Just please let me leave!"

I must have gotten on his nerves, because before long, he said, "fine, LEAVE!" I rushed for the door but all of a sudden, I felt something yank me back, and that "something" was him! He looked, laughed hysterically, and said,

"You don't get to walk out of the door! Dogs go through the doggie door," as he directed my attention to the door leading from their kitchen to the garage. Tears streamed down my eyes as I pleaded with him while resolving to get on my knees and do exactly as he commanded. The tears continued to fall, the begging continued to flow, and he continued to laugh until he soon shifted from laughter to sadness as I made my way through a hole not fit for human degradation.

Before I knew it, he was running upstairs; I retracted my movements, got up and ran behind him as a close second. He ran straight for his parents' room and slammed the door. There I stood banging and waiting for him to answer, pleading with him to forgive me for what I had not done and begging him to let me in. After a few moments, I decided to take the risk — I loved him and I had to make sure he was okay, so I opened the door. There he laid on his parents' bed, on his back, casket-style with a bible on his chest and a knife in his hand.

"Baby, please stop this," I repeated like a broken record. There he lay, just as silent as he was when I arrived. I walked closer to the bed, and continued to plead my case,

"I don't know who told you that, but I love you and would never do that to you."

As I spoke, tears began to stream down the sides of his face, as his fair complexion turned beet red. I walked up slowly, took the knife from his hand, grabbed his hands in mine and laid beside him on the floor. I didn't care what his parents would think, I didn't care if they caught us upstairs, I just needed him to be okay.

One would think that with an incident like this, and being that our relationship was just beginning, that I would go ahead and call it quits, but instead, it fueled me even more. It didn't matter how many times

I brought up what happened, he would immediately become irritated and insist that we move forward and not speak about it at all. Eventually I agreed, knowing that the wall he had created was way too big for me to overcome at that time. My love for him was crazy and it only became worse once I gave him a gift that could only be given once, my virginity. I don't know if I felt that it would make him stay with me or if I just wanted to prove how much I cared, but there came a day, after school, broad daylight in his room full of blue walls, where I surrendered who I was in that very moment. I didn't care about pregnancy or disease much less protection, I just wanted him, and to fill that crack in his heart that wanted me dead just weeks before.

Within a matter of weeks, I began feeling bad. For me, pregnancy wasn't a possibility, until I missed my cycle. I tried to explain it away, feeling noticeable changes within my body, but the truth was unescapable – I was pregnant and I knew it. Buying a pregnancy test had me looking behind my back, as I hoped and prayed that no one would see me in the store and even more, that my family would never find out. I knew that I would have denial should it be positive, so I made sure to buy more than one to confirm the results. I went into the bathroom suspecting, and within what felt like forever, it was confirmed that I was pregnant. The love I felt for this guy would cause anyone to assume that he would be my first phone call, but instead all I heard was the warning he implanted in my head,

"If you get pregnant by me and ever try to move on, I'll kill you and the baby, too."

I knew that if I kept it, I would be trapped, so I grabbed a phone book and looked up abortion clinics in the area. The day finally came for the procedure, and all I could think about was what he would say and what God would do to me, nevertheless my boyfriend's death threat took the lead. The drive to Winston-Salem was heartbreaking, as I spent the last few moments with my seed. As I arrived, everything seemed to move in slow motion — I checked in as if it was a normal doctor's appointment and sat down. I looked around the room and found some girls who were just as traumatized as me and others who were reading magazines and having whimsical conversations about what they would do once they came out of the recovery room.

"Brandi.... you can come back now."

28

I stood up, scared for my life. The lady saw it all over me.

"Don't worry, everything will be just fine."

A sigh of relief filled my lungs though my heart knew it would not be as fine as she presented. She took me into a room, a makeshift office, where she gave me a rundown of the procedure and told me what to expect. At the end of her explanation, she ended again with,

"Everything will be just fine.

You can always have more kids later."

She smiled reassuringly. I smiled back, through tears. They led me to the room and instructed me to change into a gown. As I sat in this quiet, sanitary room, the sound of machines commenced on either side of me.

No crying.

No screaming.

Just the sound of vacuums filled my ears.

Soon after the sound stopped, a middle aged man with a lab coat walked in, introduced himself and confirmed who I was. A nurse came in behind him; I remember her being really nice to me.

"Lay down and scoot your bottom down. I'm going to apply a topical injection and then we'll get started."

I looked at the nurse who again gave me a reassuring smile. The vacuum next door soon became the sound that filled my room. The procedure began and before I knew it, I gripped the nurse's hand so tight that my nails began to dig in her skin. I began to back away from the vacuum until finally, the doctor stopped and said,

"Do you really want to do this?"

I looked, shaking my head no and then responded, "yes sir, I have no choice."

The procedure concluded and they gave me instructions for the recovery room. I walked out, completely devastated about what I had just done, head down, tears streaming down my face. I exited the door but not before looking down and seeing a silver bowl with a fetus sitting inside of it, uncovered. I knew immediately that was my baby, the one I just willfully surrendered, for fear of what my boyfriend would do if I kept it. One of the attendants in the hallway saw me, unable to move, and shaking my head rapidly. They ran with a towel, covered my baby up and directed me to recovery.

Recovery post-abortion, consisted of a room full of recliner chairs, juice, crackers and women who all made the same decision. There was a girl beside me who was quiet and would not communicate with anyone, but instead would only stare at the other girls, some of which were in complete solitude while others were making plans for the club later.

"You know we're gonna be okay, right?," I asked as I petitioned for her eyes to meet mine. While it seemed that I was saying it to encourage her, I knew that I was doing it to keep me sane. I had not felt that crazy since my father died and had made plans to take my life; that moment left me saying to her what I wished someone had said to me.

My ride waited for me to come back to the waiting room. After making sure that I was okay, we walked to the car, and began to drive back to the city. I couldn't even cry, but while riding, a text came through.

"There's a game for my school tonight and we're going. Get yourself together and meet me there."

31

He didn't know what I had just done and I knew that not showing up would cause horrible consequences, so I simply replied, "okay." I arrived home and read the instructions I had received from the clinic, mainly including instructions for me to REST. I knew what the paper said, but they didn't know my boyfriend, so I sat for a while, picked out my outfit, and left to attend the football game with my man, who would have been my baby's father.

It didn't take long for me to break the news to him. Depression hit me like a ton of bricks and waking up in the morning screaming at the top of my lungs didn't help.

"WHAT? YOU DID WHAT?"

"Baby I'm sorry! You said if I ever got pregnant, that you..."

"I CAN'T BELIEVE YOU DID THIS TO ME!"

Rage filled the phone line as he took me back to the doggie door, at least in his mind. I wept more and more loudly as I recalled how every sign of a baby took me down a spiraling disaster of emotions. From children's clothing stores to babies in strollers, I never knew the moment or the incident that would set me off. It did not take long before he shifted and said,

"Let's just forget that this happened! We're going to move forward." As selfish as it was, that was music to my ears, as I was already suffering the consequences in the ministry that I had joined. (Due to my decision, I was "sat down" for six months, a period of recovery.) By this time I was ministering in dance so, that's what they took away, the ability to minster in the performing arts, and that tore my heart to shreds because it was the main thing that kept me balanced. What I knew was wrong, progressively became worse, as he would meet me at church, disapprove of my outfit, pull me outside and make me go home and change my clothes.

I remember one Sunday like it was yesterday. I had a short sleeved, red dress that I loved, and I knew that he would, too. It was a beautiful day and I was ready to praise God. I arrived shortly before he did and upon his arrival he went from smiles to anger. Immediately, I was on guard as I was preparing myself for whatever would happen next. As we walked inside the church he demanded,

"Wait. Come outside."

He then grabbed my arm and led me outside the doors while telling me that my outfit was not permitted and I had to change my clothes. At that moment, I don't know if it was his reaction that blew me away or more so, the men who saw him rough me up and refused to intervene. He then advised me that he was following me home to make sure I did as he ordered. That five-minute ride became a day of horror as I approached my mother's house. I ran inside in an attempt to avoid her inquiry,

"What are you doing here and WHY are you changing clothes?," she asked. I gave her every lie I could think of only to realize that she had already looked outside and saw "him" standing there with his arms folded. Immediately, she ran outside to confront him, telling him off in a way that I had never seen – a house coat, foam rollers, and house shoes was the attire as she told him who he was and what he didn't have a right to do. She yelled and he smirked as I walked outside, a new outfit applied. My mom looked disappointed yet confrontational as she watched me get back in my car and drive up the road with him following close behind. Within months, our relationship went from dating to being engaged. Those who didn't know about what happened between us loved him, but those who had discernment, including my pastor at the time, wouldn't bless our relationship with a five-foot pole. Eventually he built up enough audacity to be engaged to me, while pursuing a relationship with another young lady while we were all in the same space at any given time and she was game! I even had people who realized what was happening praying that we would break up!

So, there we were, Father's Day 1998 and my father had only been gone for four years. I asked if he would accompany me to the cemetery to pay my respects and surprisingly, he agreed. I led the way as he drove behind me; weeping filled my car as I drove still stunned by my reality. As we approached, I got out of the car slowly, bracing myself for the emotions that would pour out of my soul. My then fiancé' came up behind me, walked past me, got down on the ground and sat on my father's grave Indian-style, with a smile on his face. In that moment, all fear left me and rage became my friend as I demanded that he tell me what he was doing and even more, that he get up! There he sat, snickering as if he had won the most competitive chess match ever created and there I stood over him, tapping into a feeling I had suppressed for well over a year.

"GET UP! MOVE!"

He wouldn't budge.

"You know what? This is IT! I'm done!

I'm through! It's over!"

My heart broke and moved with the song of freedom as I headed back to my car. He jumped up, throwing all kinds of insults and even ran and took my cell phone out of my car.

"HA!," he yelled, "you won't leave without this!"

"Take it," I yelled back, " I would rather be without a phone than be with you ANY DAY!"

This day, I broke out of my prison. This day I launched into freedom. This time in my life was marked, from altar to alter; as I did on the cold slab that day in October 1997, I knew that that there was no alternative; there was no other choice.

2.

Envisioning the Call

God has a way that is mighty sweet, these are the sentiments that often flood my mind. Man looks at us and deems us unqualified, while God looks at us and says, "they're just right for the job!" After reading the last chapter, one would think that God wouldn't call me to preach His gospel after a fiasco like that, but that's exactly when He did it! Yes, there were signs, as I think back to being twelve and even thirteen years old with a karaoke mic in one hand along with a bible and the mirror on my nightstand serving as my congregation. Or maybe, it was the times that I would play church with my friends, only to always end up being a good pew member or maybe a greeter but NEVER the minister (that would tear my nerves up!) So instead, I would go home and preach to myself.

Those seeds eventually turned into embers and later fire, as I continued to attend church, recover and realize that God still had a future designed just for me. This confirmation did not come through angels filling my room etc., but instead through dreams that flooded my times of rest. These visions became so strong that there was no way that I could deny their existence, nor the pull to follow what I saw. I confided it in one individual, an Elder at the church who had adopted me in his family because I was just that tight with his niece, Daph. When I told him what God was calling me to, his face lit up, and celebration became his reply. Let me be honest - he was also the only Elder to find out about the abortion, so to watch him celebrate at this moment blew my mind. I thought that my "newfound call," was a conversation between us, but it took a Sunday morning to realize that the news had spread like wildfire.

"We have someone here today, who has accepted their call to preach the gospel. Brandi, stand up!"

People all around me began praising God as I stood, shocked that they would even acknowledge me, after all, this was a mega church and I didn't know any women there who was preaching under this affiliation of people. Yes there were missionaries, but I knew that God was calling me to a different arena and despite the announcement, I was not even close to ready. So, do you remember the karaoke machine I told you about earlier? Well, it never crossed my mind that maybe, just maybe, God was setting me up.

In my mind, I was just rehearsing what I had watched for years, but God was birthing something greater on the inside of me.

This confession took me back to an incident that happened at the church I grew up in, the manifestation of dreams and visions. At that time in my life, I did not have a Google page or search engine that I could go to and type in the words,

"What does it mean when you see a mysterious "light" show up in your grandmother's hospital room?"

Ok, allow me to explain. When I was around sixteen years old, my mother let me know that my grandmother, her mother, would have to go through surgery for a leg amputation. This news came after an encounter that happened in her room. That day, no one was in the room. I remember cracking the door open, and seeing her asleep, did my very best to creep in and not wake her. She rested, as I calmly walked up to her. My grandmother, also named Norma (my mother is named after her) had the most beautiful, silver grey hair. I am sure that when she got her hair done, others in the room probably wanted what she had. Its length went below her neckline, and it was the softest hair, probably ever created. There I stood at the foot of her bed, with nothing on in the room except the faint sound of the television in the background. I stood and observed for what had to be a few minutes, and then something strange happened — the television faded black, and all of a sudden, a glow came from under her bed and hovered over her leg. I have to laugh because moments like this remind me of horror movies where we yell at the screen, "GET OUT OF THERE," but the character stands, completely shocked, while Jason comes up with his funky music to take them out. Seriously, I could not move, and even if I could, I wouldn't. One of the key things that I noticed was that even though it was the craziest thing I had ever seen, it brought a peace with it that I could not deny. So, there it hovered, and there I stood, until it finally disappeared. Though I cannot recall what day that was, one thing was for sure, I could not wait until Sunday showed up.

The morning came and all I could think about was what happened in that hospital room. In my mind, I would go to church and my Pastor would say something to bring clarity to everything I had seen. I sat through the entire service and listened to a powerful word. As always, the altar call came and people came up for salvation and prayer. They prayed for the people, and while they did I shot up like a blade of grass and rushed up to the front. As they were preparing to transition, I asked for the microphone and without hesitation, gained access. I stood before the congregation, feeling in my gut that either one of two things would happen – either they would think I was crazy or it would cause some indescribable praise break. As you can imagine, I told my testimony and you could literally hear a pen drop. I dropped my head, handed the microphone back to the minister and returned to my seat. This day I realized that what God had done with me was unusual and that maybe my calling was more than I or even those around me could handle.

As we get back to this life changing announcement, my calling was declared and people began praising the Lord. From that moment I knew that I was marked though I did not know how that would transform. Within the first few years at that ministry, I went from being a dance vessel to the dance choreographer for the youth department which later became an outreach ministry. I had a desire to dance in church, but did not pursue it at first, but instead, it pursued me. I was approached by a strong, New York accented woman one day by the name of Mary Stevens; I later discovered, that she was the mother of a few of my classmates from school. Somehow, whether by her children or other means, she discovered that I danced, too. One day after church I found myself in a conversation, after introduction, that sounded something like this:

"Hey Baby! Let me ask you something – have you ever danced for Jesus?"

"No ma'am."

"Well baby, you do now!"

Yes, that is how the door of worship dance opened up for me. It was there that I learned the importance of hard word, dedication and why liturgical dance laid so heavily on my heart. I gained family, some of which I am still connected to this day, all while stepping into a depth of dance I never imagined. For me, dance up until that point had become about technical skill and proficiency, but there was something about the ministry of dance that caught my attention. As a choreographer, I found myself dancing everywhere, even in the car as I drove. I was a whole high school student, but willing to drive wherever I had to go to minister in dance. There were times that people would watch and not say a word, and other times where complete deliverance would break out, but I was there for it all. I knew that through the art of dance, I was breaking walls that I could not even see and defeating enemies and demonic forces that I could not even name. The weight of my footsteps and the rhythm in my movements was crushing the head of the enemy, and I did not even realize it.

3.

BLACKBALLED

Blackballed:

"the rejection of someone usually by means of a secret ballot."

As a young person on fire for the Lord, you expect the best of all things as it relates to the church and your relationship with the Lord, but that is simply not true. As with life and the world, the church is an organism of its own, filled with miracles, signs, wonders, with conflicts and heartache, too. Even as I share this portion of my story with you, I do so taking deep, intentional breaths, as I share this from the recesses of my soul.

There I was, having had an abortion, but God still chose to use me. As you may be feeling as you read this, I could not make sense of it either, nevertheless I remained grateful as I pursued His presence. I was a girl whose parents divorced when I was five years old. There was never any preparation for that loss and no conversation that I can remember. For years, I stayed with my grandparents mostly, and when I was not there, I was at home. I became a daddy's girl quickly, so his passing when I was only fourteen came with its own challenges from anger to regret and more. My brother, though he was nine years older than me, tried his best to protect me, but he could never take the place of my daddy. All I really wanted was my daddy, period. As any little girl would, I was not fully aware of any shortcomings that would cause me to remove myself as the president of his fan club. Sunday after Sunday, I would watch how my Pastor treated his daughter and wish for that kind of moment, just one more time, but knowing that moment would never be mind again. So many moments that he would never be there for – he missed my prom; he would miss my getting married, choosing a career and even having children. For the life of me, I could not make sense of why God took my father when He did and forced me to simply accept what He allowed.

Let me be honest, for me, being blackballed or even a "black sheep" did not start as an adult but instead the moment I found myself going through places that according to "my plan" should not have happened to me. For years I sought out people to fill the missing space, thus the previous abusive relationship I was in that I just shared with you. As I continued to pursue a relationship with God, there were some spaces that I would not even allow Him to fill, that I would not even allow Him to touch.

At the age of twenty-one, I decided to move out of my mother's house and get a roommate; her name was Raleta and she was super dope! She was always energetic, scholastic and an overall sweet girl. We met at work and became instant friends and shortly thereafter, decided that we would get an apartment together. Within about four months, we were cool but knew that it would not work. There were days that she witnessed me with another guy at the apartment. I am not saying that something happened with them, but yes, there were a few, as I carried the ailing desire of a space-filler, even living in a new place.

Despite my indecencies, God never stopped warning or dealing with me. I remember one day, I was sitting and felt that I needed to begin looking for another place to stay. By the next day, we had a conversation and it was confirmed. Gratefully, it did not take long for me to find another place; in fact it probably took longer for me to justify such a swift move to my mother. New places, new spaces, and still there I was, taking "myself" wherever I went. Hear me, God was still using me, directing me, and even favoring me, all while I gave pieces of me out in hopes of finding someone who spoke the same language to repair something in me that they did not even break. It was also within this same year, that God instructed me to find my grandfather on my father's side. For me, it seemed pointless, since I had only met him once and that was at my father's funeral. He was the sweetest man indeed, but he promised he would be there and from the day of the funeral until the day I stood in, I had not seen him. Despite the record I tried to present before God, I finally obeyed. I don't know "how" I found him – I promise you that it was only God.

The day I located him, I was advised that he was in the hospital. I called, and my uncle who I would later know as Uncle Gad, answered. "Hello," he answered. I quickly returned the sentiment and told him who I was. "Nate! Nate's daughter! Nehemiah, it's your granddaughter, Nathaniel's daughter." I prepared myself, excited to hear my grandfather's voice after so many years. I heard a faint attempt to speak and then a heavy breath, and finally chaos filled the room. It was then that I realized he had died with me on the phone. There I sat unable to cry over a man I had never had the opportunity in my soul, all while never realizing that the mantle on his life had just been transferred to me. This reality would years down the road, be solidified within me, without question.

It's something when you make your request known, but forget that just as God hears, the enemy does, too. There I was at school one day, on Blackplanet.com, and up pops a profile called, "DaLastGoodMan." He was out of state, which intrigued me. Somehow, someway, we spoke and that conversation turned into a relationship and transformed into a Greyhound bus ride, and engagement, and later a marriage. Let me be clear, we both came from broken homes and came together, broken, so needless to say, we accomplished much but was like a train wreck waiting to happen. I tried to be the best wife I could, and I believe he tried his best based on what he knew to do. It is amazing how many believe that just because there is a ceremony, both people come with an automatic "Husband/Wife Switch," that makes us absolutely perfect and proficient at being a spouse. Oh, if the marriage had remained as beautiful as the ceremony, but life happened.

I remember like it was yesterday, the church envelopes filled with change and the scotch tape that held it together; you see, it was all we had to sow in church and oftentimes embarrassment led the way as the one holding the bucket would always bend down a bit when we approached. If not, I would always make sure that when we put our change in the bucket, we would gently lay the envelope down in the receptacle praying no one would notice. Every time I did it, the voice of one of my Pastors growing up, Pastor Rosa, would resound through, "God don't want to hear the sound of change, only the sound of bills," but it was all I had to give and I could only pray that God respected it.

Sunday after Sunday we did this, and Sunday after Sunday people whispered and even laughed. Why you ask? It wasn't because of the envelope but instead, because as time went on I began to grow out of my regular clothes as I carried the blessing of the life that existed within me, our son. I would walk by with my growing belly and watch key members from the praise team who I deeply admired, snicker and laugh; the moment I made eye contact with them, they would immediately straighten up and attempt to shut their conversations off with, "I'm sorry," amongst more giggles.

There came a moment when I realized that enough was enough, and that was the day that one person decided to say what everyone wouldn't,

"Girl you need to get some maternity clothes!"

I could only stand still and look as she waited for my reaction. I pondered for a moment and said,

"Well if it bothers you, buy me some because this is all I have and I don't have the money to

buy anything else."

Thankfully, someone heard my cry some weeks later and showed up with exactly what I needed. This would not serve as the first time that this would happen for me, but all along the way God continued to prove Himself to us despite the challenges we faced.

I had to be about five months the day when I found myself standing before a borderline empty refrigerator. I looked around in the cabinets but couldn't find anything that I really wanted in that moment. This was the stint of time when Cici's Pizza was everything and surely, it was just that to me. To have five dollars to go and eat all of the salad, pizza and breadsticks I wanted was a pregnant woman's dream that became reality and brought me supreme joy; on the other hand there was those other days when life was not so kind and left me wondering what I would have to re-create to survive. No matter the "community resources," one would imagine was available, we walked away with the determination that we made "too much," though our life as a whole said otherwise. There I stood before the refrigerator, wondering what to do. I couldn't figure it out, so out of frustration I began talking to it — yes, I talked to it. I began to say out loud what I wanted to see — everything from turkey, to dressing, collard greens, macaroni and cheese, the whole nine. With my face full of tears, I eventually closed the fridge, knowing in the words of my mother, that keeping it open was wasting the cold air.

We only had one car and so as usual, I looked at my watch and realized that it was time to go. I didn't even have time to forward anyone my "dream list," which is why the phone call I received was so surprising to me.

Hey Brandi.

Hey, what's up?

I'm at the store and wanted to know if you were home.

No, but I will be soon.

Ok, I'm going to get you a few items and leave them at your door.

Ok, yes ma'am. Thank you!

I rushed home – I had no idea what was waiting on me, but it had to be better than what I had. I could see the brown grocery bags from the street and as I approached, I began weeping. Every single thing I asked God for was right there on my doorstep – every item I spoke, was right there. Grateful was an understatement, indeed. This was just one instance that God showed up for us, just one.

We went through love together, lack together and out of that union was born a baby boy, the most beautiful blessing of our union, weighing a little over six pounds named Malachi. As a baby, and even now eighteen years later, his smile could brighten any room, and cause any argument-produced tears to quickly fade away. It didn't matter what we went through, that chocolate blessing of mine always caused me to remember that our fight was no longer for us but for him. As time progressed, we were eventually blessed to have a home built from the ground up. During that time, there was something happening in the economy called a "balloon mortgage," which was approving families for homes but would later skyrocket mortgages to a rate that could not be announced, well, until you got first mortgage bill after your first year in the home. (A federal lawsuit was later initiated which produced a settlement check in the amount of $300.00, no more, no less.) In that moment, we remained optimistic, thinking that maybe this move would be the one to solidify us and cause us not to be at each other's throats. In our minds, or at least mine, this move would at least make us look more like a couple, right? Surely, this house with custom everything would fix the problem and cause every person who doubted our success to eat their words, too. So, we did it, we bought a house, we moved in, and life, love and eventually what began to feel like hell, commenced.

From 2006 to 2009, there were many amazing days, but the bad days choked out the memory. He was Husband and I was Wife, but our partnership was completely frayed. As time progressed, it felt like we had a constant cloud that hung over our house while sunshine beamed on all of the others around us. We had a beautiful home on the outside and praised God for every day that seemed to feel at least halfway normal. I repeat, we praised God – meaning, we were involved in ministry. I was dancing with the dance ministry, we were involved in the marriage ministry and I even eventually became part of a teaching program at our church where I was one of nineteen graduates out of over one hundred who started with us.

All of this happened, while our home was falling apart, hearts were being broken, nervous breakdowns became normal and overall, life was happening. After failed attempts at attending Real Estate school, I had decided that maybe it was time for a change altogether, maybe it was time for me to go back to school. Just as quickly as I made the decision, I spoke to my job, shifted from full-time to part time, applied at my dream school (UNC-Greensboro) and awaited their reply. The application process was quite detailed and even required an on-site interview. As I sat across from the admissions department, I saw in their hands my application, on which I had written in tiny letters at the bottom, Ephesians 3:20. In my mind, I NEEDED God to do this for me, and I was determined to get in. Within a week I found out that I had been admitted, and just like that I was a wife, mom, part-time employee, and full-time college student, majoring in Dance with minors in Business Administration and Psychology.

There is a saying that goes like this, "when it rains, it pours." Though I do not ascribe to this belief now (it opens too much "opportunity,") at that moment in time it felt like that was the only way to describe where I was. Heartbreak became the norm as words were exchanged and actions, too, none of which became healing for either of our souls. I felt that being in school would help me to at least feel that I could do something right, but eventually that began to look like my marriage, too. I will never forget the moment he went away for the weekend for a retreat and came back "a changed man." He walked in the door and rushed over to hug me, but I refused. A brother of the church walked over and said,

"Sister, I know this is hard for you to understand, but God did something for him on that mountain," to which I quickly replied,

"He went to the mountain, I didn't."

Eventually I went to the mountain, too. At first, I thought I was okay, until after the first night I found myself purging in my room, unable to sleep or get any rest. The next morning, I came downstairs and was greeted by one of our deliverance retreat guides. She saw the look on my face and immediately asked, "Brandi, what's wrong?" With tears in my eyes I told her everything I felt to which she gently and nonchalantly replied, "Oh, that's rage. We'll deal with that in a bit." I stood, stunned, knowing that though I was aware of "grudge holding" being a part of my bloodline, rage had never come up. As promised, as praise and worship commenced, and with tons of women in the room, the ministers began to pull a few ladies here and a few ladies there, one being me. That day, we went through our own levels of deliverance — mine was filled with lots of "carpet ministry," and at the worst, foaming at the mouth. When I came to, what I remembered felt like it had happened to someone else but it was confirmed, it was me. We came back home and life was good, at least for a little while.

Over time, I adjusted and resolved to simply put everything contrary to survival away. I packed each memory in compartments, just enough to keep a record but not enough to go crazy, picked up my face and my pride and continued life, after all, I was never taught by anyone to react any differently. Dreams and visions became my bread and water, as I woke up many nights in cold sweats afraid of the next move and the next loss. I would ride around the city, feel something, call my ex-husband to confirm and be spot on. I continued to look for ways to cope, and for us to become the power couple I had heard so much about, but the dreams, visions and ultimate realities would not let me be great. So, my list was formed....

I went to Real Estate school twice — nervous breakdown.

I went back to college and was elevated to senior level classes but was quickly suspended when I fell 0.061 below my minimum GPA requirement.

I opened a dance studio — closed it within two months.

It seemed as if everything I tried to have what God showed me was failing all around me. I did not know about the depths of warfare, much less what it meant to have people conduct meetings about you before this happened. Even when I had my studio, people would come by and excitement would fill my soul. Little did I know that they were coming to scope out what I had going on, and go back to their meetings to place bets on my losing it. They would come in one by one, touching the walls and commenting on how beautiful the space was, laugh, giggle and all of a sudden leave without another word. Within weeks, I received a notification that the owner was demanding $25,000 for me to be able to stay. I didn't have it — in fact, I had used my school refund check just to be able to get in the space and based on my rental amount did not even owe close to that amount, nevertheless there I was, left with only two options, finding the money, or moving out.

The day I moved out of my dance studio was absolutely devastating. I told my husband at the time that I did not want help, but instead needed to do it on my own. One day, while I was taking curtains down, a lady came in holding a flyer that she had received from the parade we promoted during a parade that took place a few months earlier. She came in, puzzled and asking what I was doing.

"Ma'am we are shutting down this location."

She looked, paused then snickered and said, "Wow, that was fast," and while she left grabbed her phone to make a call. I could not cry or even scream; the loss felt like death. The losses one after the other felt like an intentional blackball that God did not even attempt to stop. I stayed at the studio that night pacing the floor and hoping, that maybe someone with the money would just show up. I walked around, praying that someone would hear my cry and just handle the need. The pacing quickly turned into desperation as I walked in circles in the dark hearing nothing but my prayers hit the ceiling. I continued to worship and beg until I heard His voice,

"Worship Me."

Knowing that God could not possibly be serious, I continued to beg, cry and pace. His voice resounded,

"Worship Me like you did when you got this place."

Immediately my mind went back in time to the moments before I was approved. I would drive to the back of the building, worship God in my car and wake up outside my car, face down on the concrete. From the depths of my soul, I let out the weakest, "Thank You Lord" I could muster. The exit light served as my only light source as I made my way to the floor.

Thank You God.

Thank You Lord.

Hallelujah.....

...filled my thoughts and my atmosphere. I worshiped so hard and for so long, that I knew that if I opened my eyes I would be staring at the feet of Jesus. After I was done, I got up, walked to the front door, locked it, grabbed the doors and whispered,

"Stay here. I'll be back."

I had no idea that shortly after graduation from the leadership program at my church, that I would find myself within two months realizing that my marriage was over, and within the same breath, that our home was going into active foreclosure. In my eyes, no act of service, ministry or prayer meant anything, because if it did, why on earth would God allow that to happen to me, and especially our household.

Despite the loss, I kept going, or at least I tried to. I became the face of embarrassment; dealing with all that was happening was bad enough, but there was nothing like the public humiliation that came with it in the place that I deemed as being safe, the church. The dance ministry had a ministry date on the books, and I, being the number two for so long, became number one by default. I was not confident, as the one who I served under always made sure that I knew that I would never be her. As I reflect, I remember a rehearsal one day, where I made a suggestion. She wouldn't even look at me, but in front of the dance team, instead said with a growl in her voice,

"Why don't you just shut up and find the CD!"

A room full of dancers and even parents stopped in their tracks. I had no one to defend me, nor the audacity to defend myself, so I did as she asked, I wiped my face, found the CD and hit play. The dance ministry saw me go through that but nothing trumped the news that had spread like wildfire among the areas of ministry in which we served and yes, even within the dance ministry itself. A beautiful, young dancer approached me one night,

"Ms. Brandi, we heard about what's going on in your house. You can quit if you want – we can find someone else."

The tears I held burned, as I did all I could not to react, knowing that my place of safety no longer was that at all, but instead, a place of demise. I could not tell who was for me or against me, and receiving confirmation of conversations about me taking place in hair salons and even at dinner tables made being stabbed seem like a supreme compliment. Home was no longer safe, and the day we moved out proved just that even the more.

There I was, cleaning out my refrigerator with tears streaming uncontrollably. The lights were beaming, as blotches of time were lost until I finally realized that another nervous breakdown had come to join the "party." Blackouts took over my body as I would go out and then regain consciousness on the floor. This time though, all I felt was the desire to die; in my mind I was a horrible wife and mom too, so dying would be a favor and an act of heroism. I reached for the phone and made a call to a ministry leader who I served with:

"Hey, I need your help."

"What's going on?"

"I want to die."

"I feel like I may just go ahead and die."

"Girl, you ain't gonna die! Listen, I'm doing something right now but I promise to call you back, okay?"

"Okay."

Hours passed, and they never called; years have passed and that call still has never come. Safety no longer meant anything as it had all, in my eyes, been taken away. All I knew was to make sure that my son was okay, that was my only consistent goal and accomplishment. Matter of fact, home became an apartment on the third floor of an apartment complex. It was so much "not home" to me, that I wouldn't even sleep in the bed but instead, I would sleep as if I were homeless on the living room floor with a pallet and my clothes on. I would put Malachi to bed in his room then leave and ride aimlessly for hours just to get away. Within weeks, I knew it was time for us to leave. I had held on way too long to a union that had proved to be disastrous, heartbreaking and turned me into someone I never imagined that I would be. I couldn't recover from all that had happened and knowing that some things were still happening within our marriage killed me a little more every day. Other married women in my circle told me that I should just suck it up and stay, but when I asked the hard questions about what they would do, crickets and rats releasing on cotton balls responded more loudly than they. As I did with my roommate, I searched for a place for us to move, just my son and I and even through that process God graced us. There I was with no consistent job or income, being approved for an apartment. In fact, as they said, they were giving me a chance, and for me that's all I needed.

Things were looking up – I was moved in and was preparing to get Malachi ready for kindergarten, but one thing escaped me, the cycle. My parents divorced when I was five years old, and there I sat looking at a little boy, who had just turned five, try to process the fact that his parents were no longer together and that he would only see his father on the weekends. Like my story, my ex and I never sat our son down and explained to him together what was happening – I guess we just assumed that since he was a kid, his resiliency would be impeccable and he would just adjust. I had to hide depression from him, just to survive and when he would catch me crying I would blame it on anything else I could think of. I promised his father, my ex, that I would never lay the weight of what happened to us on our son, and that was a promise that I had every intention on keeping; little did I know that years down the road, he would find out through a family member everything that had taken place during a period of time that he was too young to understand, thus continuing another cycle.

I applied for a job and literally received the offer on the brink of my unemployment ending. Training for my job was a breeze, until I came home one day and found my lights disconnected. I called, optimistic, just knowing it was a mistake, but it wasn't, as I was advised that the bill from my foreclosed home had never been paid to the tune of over $600.00. I wept, but not before calling my mother. She rushed over asking ALL of the questions, but all I could do was ask her to take my son while I stayed at the apartment.

"But Brandi, there's no lights."

"I know Mama, just let me go through this."

My mom ended up paying the bill for me, with the notification that they would not be out for three days.

Three days.

No lights.

Food moved to a friend's house.

No hot water.

Just candles, me, and my recovery.

One night, perplexed as I was, I forgot that I had left my keys in the door. There I was in the dark with nothing but a few candles lit. There was a knock at the door; I wasn't expecting anyone so I merely hoped that they just had the wrong apartment. I opened the door to find the guy who lived upstairs, I could tell by the looks of him that he was high on something, but definitely not on life. He said, "Yoooo! My bad, I didn't mean to disturb your mood candles, but I saw your keys in the door and wanted to let you know." I smiled, thanked him as he walked away saying, "Tell dude or girl, whoever's in there, my bad." This guy thought that I was creating a mood! He thought that I was in there with "company." I laughed as I closed the door, and I told them I would make "them" aware. "Duke, he said he's sorry babe," I yelled to pacify his request. (Duke Energy was our service provider just in case you're wondering how I came up with a name that quickly.) Three days passed, and I survived it; once they reconnected my lights, I pledged that I would NEVER go through that again, not realizing that the enemy was after a whole different source of light that money could not supply.

THE CLUB

4.

THE GREAT ESCAPE

So, there I was — a single parent, a new apartment, having completely disconnected from my church home, just sitting, waiting for the next step of this new life. I cannot call it fate, but right before my son and I moved, I discovered this nifty website called "Facebook." Hurt led my fingertips as I quickly went to the page I had created with my married name and reverted my name back to my maiden name; I was done and I wanted the world to know it.

It wasn't long before I started reconnecting with people online. People from my past were coming through a mile a minute and I was loving every minute of it. For me, it became my escape, as I worked to adjust to life after marriage, hurt, pain, and rage. One day while online, I received a communication from an old friend. Immediately, I was excited because after all, it was my homegirl from middle school and I was sure that she would strengthen my efforts to forget what I had just come out of. Our conversation turned into an invitation to go out, and without hesitation, I said, "YES." After all, my son would be with his father and I had not had the opportunity to go out for a girl's night in years. I looked around realizing that I didn't have a thing to wear; if we were just going out to eat I would be fine, but I know that this "going out," would require me to look the part.

The night came, and I was so excited. There I was, hair molded down, heels strapped up and my hot pink, strapless dress from Charlotte Russe on ready to take on the night. You know, it was the kind of dress that wouldn't permit me to drop anything and pick up it up unless, well you get my point. I was a whole snack and I knew it. What amazed me was that I felt completely comfortable. For years modest dress was my thing, but in this moment, I felt sexy, desirable, different. I gathered up my "coins" to make sure I was completely together from head to toe. The French manicure on my feet was everything even down my individual lashes, makeup, and my French tips. My goal was complete — to look as if nothing ever happened and that despite what I had accepted, any man would have been lucky to have me on his arm.

The first night was something special. I came in apprehensive but tried to hide it. My homegirl on the other hand was a pro as she knew who was who, knew what to order and exactly what to do to make the most of the evening. I watched her and even went on the dance floor with her once or twice. Like a deer in headlights, I was afraid to move, but figured that I would at least make my presence known. I had not taken a drink in years, but the cups and the bottles all around me made the decision easy. At first, it was just to be social, but I noticed, the more I drank the more loose I felt and ultimately the more quiet the voices in my head became. I did not do much of anything that night outside of a couple of drinks, a bounce here or there and meeting some new people. In my eyes, my homegirl, Tasha, had become my new best friend, and the one who would help lead me out of this perpetual heartbreak that I found myself in.

One thing I learned about me early on was that alcohol had the ability to relax me but no matter how much I drank, it never caused a "morning after" reaction. I had never had a hangover, and even in this newfound freedom, that truth had not changed. Whether or not my drinks "went together" was of little importance, as I drank, bounced, and bopped my head all to do it all over again the very next weekend. When the $1 promos were popping off, I knew that Heineken and a Hurricane would be my drinks of choice. Chasing them one after the other became my specialty; with those two on my team, I felt like I couldn't lose. This combination gave me guts like I had never seen or had before. My audacity was at an all time high, I wasn't afraid to approach anyone and I surely wasn't afraid to tell anyone about themselves.

Drinking followed me from the club to the house, and just as like the club, I didn't care who saw what I was picking up. At home, beer wasn't my purchase, but instead red wine, specifically, Dublin, was. I don't know how I even discovered it, outside of just wanting some kind of fancy buzz periodically during the week. After putting my son to bed, I made it my business to grab a glass and sit on the balcony of my apartment. In those moments, the cool breeze would flow through my deck and for once life began to feel normal. I went from one glass a night to a whole bottle in one sitting when my son was not around. I recall one time, where I was so drunk that my oldest goddaughter, Keyona, had to put me in the bed and lock my door when she left. I had known by way of my own family what alcoholism could cause, as it was how my father became disabled several years before he passed, but none of that matters in the face of disaster and pain.

Alcohol became my savior.

Alcohol became my escape.

Alcohol became my new love.

Alcohol, in those moments, made the voices disappear.

In that moment, Alcohol, became my peace.

5.

DUFFLE BAGS AND
WARDROBE CHANGES

Life shifted quickly, and despite the minor bumps in the road, the adjustment was well, adjusting. Shortly after training at my new job, I received the news of my official work schedule. Prior to the latter part of our training, I pleaded with our trainer to have a schedule that would work with my new found status of "single mom," to which they obliged. It wasn't until the schedule came out that I realized that despite my situation, I would have to make a major decision, asking my mother to help with my son. I looked down at the paper which stated,

3:00pm – 11:00pm, Monday/Tuesday off.

I didn't know what to say as I knew that I NEEDED this job, so thankfully my mother, who was retired by this time, agreed to help me. Every Wednesday and Thursday she would pick up my son from school and care for him until I got off work, then on Sundays until I was released to go home. Friday evenings through Sunday evenings, my son would visit with his father. In that moment I guess the upside to that arrangement was that I never had to see my ex, but instead simply had to be ready to care for my son when he returned.

More than anything, I wanted things to be normal for my baby boy, or at least as normal as could be. I smile as I reflect on the day he went away for the weekend and returned to our apartment to find that his room had been transformed into a Spider Man room! The look on his face was priceless as he ran down the hallway screaming, "THANK YOU, MOMMY!" Moments like this gave me joy because I knew that I was finally making some pivotal moves and adjustments that were working. Even down to him going into kindergarten, these are moments that constantly flood my mind. The first day of school, I found myself walking him to the door fast, and walking away even faster, as I had determined within myself that I would not become a victim of the 1st day of school cry-a-thon! As I ensured that his teacher had him and prepared to turn around, he yelled, "Mommy," and took off running down the hallway into my arms. I grabbed him and took the deepest breath ever determined that we were going to be just fine.

So I seemed to have the Best Mom award on lock, but on the inside I was suffering. A one time occasion at the club turned into an every weekend,

Friday through Sunday, event; I mean, a new outfit every week until I had them in rotation, new lashes every two weeks, nails always done and never lifting, toes flawless. It didn't take long before I became a part of "the crew," and security at the front door recognized who I was. I went from being my childhood friend's "quiet friend," to her bodyguard. I could discern who needed to be around her when she couldn't tell or simply was not paying attention, how many ice cubes needed to be in her drink, what she wanted to drink and even remove her out of environments in case a borderline altercation broke out. This was the place, believe it or not, that God used to train me as an Armor Bearer.

This responsibility required me to be ready to show up at the club, not at 1:00am in the morning but instead, the moment they opened or as close as I could get to it. Now keep in mind, it opened at 10:00pm and the price went up at 11:00pm. I knew that I would be late because of my work schedule so what better way was there to make it there without missing more than I needed to? The only answer was my black duffle bag.

My duffle bag for years consisted of ballet shoes and praise dance attire but had now become the safe haven for mini-dresses and stilettos. Friday afternoons consisted of figuring out what I as going to wear to the club that night. Mostly consisting of super short dresses, heels, baby oil, body spray, deodorant and makeup, I stayed on ready. My last break at work was around 10:00pm. I would go to the bathroom, put my club dress on over my leggings etc., along with my shoes. I would oil my legs up, freshen up my face and make it back to my desk within fifteen minutes. As soon as 10:55pm popped up, I would immediately go into aftercall, because I was determined not to get caught on the phone and miss out on my club fix. 11:00pm would hit and I would run out the door, all gas no breaks, jump in the car, take off my leggings, start my car and was in the wind. It didn't matter how cold it was outside, all I wanted was my moment to get away from it all. I just wanted to be able to get to the place where my escape existed.

For me, the club was like fresh air. There I could be anyone I wanted to be, or so I thought. You see, as much as I tried to get away from the stigma of the "church girl," I always found myself being pulled in that direction. Whether it was someone who needed me to pray for protection before we walked in a club, being tugged on to teach some un-coordinated person how to dance, or praying as we sat around a table full of food so drunk that we couldn't stand, the God in me was always being pulled on. It did not matter how many men I slept with or how many drinks I took down, God's voice remained loud in my ears.

Wardrobe changes for me went far beyond going from work to the party scene for the weekend — it even included sneaking in an out of places before the crack of dawn. I recall a friend of mine having a birthday party and inviting me. Immediately, I asked about her brother who I dated when we were merely teenagers. She confirmed that he would be there and my face lit up, wondering how he would react when he saw me walk in. That night I went all out and came through with more of everything — more smile, more strut, more sweet talk, more everything. As I approached I even made sure the way I spoke sounded melodious yet nonchalant, knowing that I had no intention on making him believe that did all of that for him though I did. All night I danced and chilled, drank and caught up with his family but kept an eagle eye on him. As the night concluded, he approached me; I could tell what he wanted by the look in his eyes and I was down for it. We exchanged numbers and left with plans to link up within a couple of hours. I wasted no time getting myself together as I prepared for the moment we never had as teens. Phone tag became the name of the game and that night never materialized, but it did not take long to catch up. Nights would come while I was overtaken by club lights and would see his name come across my phone. I would smile big as day, knowing what that meant. My plan was to play in the pond, but within a few encounters I began to catch feelings. We weren't just limited to sex, but even our intellectual conversations caused one another to see other sides of us that we liked, or at least, I liked. I felt that we were going somewhere, until the night came when he let me know his true intent.

Showing up at his place was never a problem until one night when he opened the door and put one finger over his lips. "Shhhh," he said, "my kids are here." That night happened but was restricted for obvious reasons. The deed was done but I knew that pillow talk this time wasn't an option. As usual, he helped me zip up my dress, but as I reached for my heels he said, "No, don't put those on. You'll make too much noise. I don't need my kids to wake up much less see you." I looked, frowning yet accepting, because after all it was his house and his kids, right? There I was, dress on, hair disheveled and no shoes, creeping out of his apartment, down the stairs and on the cold, hard parking lot below. That night, he did not even wait for me to get to my car as usual, but instead closed the door as soon as I began walking down the hall. There was no check-in to make sure I arrived home. I messaged him, but needless to say, he didn't reply.

One would think that after an exchange like that, that you would get the point and just leave the man be, but not me. Yes, I was still hurt, but for me, this rekindled moment felt like potential. Some days I would call and he would sound completely engaged; other days would call and he would sound completely detached. He would still reach out for our "sessions," and I would show up without fail, after all, he was trying to get a release and I was trying to forget my life. One night, I made a proposition that we go out and get a bite to eat at a nearby restaurant called Ham's. He fought the idea but I continued to pitch and even beg him to come. I remember my words,

"Listen, I will pay you to go out in public with me. Let's just go eat, okay?"

Finally, whether it be by desire or me getting on his nerves he agreed and I was satisfied with that. He requested a table near the door. Every time it opened, he looked up as if he was expecting someone. I don't know how many times I asked if he was okay, but every time he replied that he was fine. Regardless of all of the signs, I was determined to be Beyonce' and Jay Z 2.0, yes just me (B) and he, (J). I finally had to admit that I had fallen in love with someone who had never loved me. Reality hit that same night as I brought up my son and his children. His response was cold and uncaring,

"I'm trying to deal with you and do what we do, but I don't want to meet your son and I don't want him to meet me, either."

Again, there I sat, rejected and alone, but this time, without a ring. I couldn't cry because there was no point - I had fallen for the game that I thought I had perfected and as a result, crushed my own heart. To this day, he probably does not realize how much that moment hurt me. In my mind we could have spent a couple of forevers, but in his, we were nothing more than a few come and goes.

6.

SKIP LINES

One thing I learned early was that skip lines made you look rich, favored or both. Even if you only had to pay $20, being able to walk through the skip line made you look like you were something special. Loud music and deceiving lighting filled the space, but who cares about that when you can get past that by way of a few drinks? For me, it didn't matter if a dude was ugly or anything otherwise, I wanted what I wanted, to quiet the voices and finally be free.

I met a lot of females, but a lot of men, too. I don't know if they understood the hurt I was in, but neither of us were vested to that degree, so encounters were just that, encounters. I never "crossed over," but the opportunity had presented itself multiple times to which I replied, "flattered but declining." Early on, a man approached me and by the end of the night he had my phone number and address. I knew what he wanted and I was down, after all, if the next five minutes of my life could further my cause, I was for it. So, we tried, and it was horrible.

Maybe it was because we were on the floor.

Maybe it was because we were strangers.

Either way, it was horrible for sure.

From that day, I never feared anyone having my address. I never assumed that someone I was dealing with long or short term would do anything that drastic. After being tossed by my teenage love, I had decided that I would never fall for that game again, but instead, that I would run the game myself. Everything about me changed; I tucked Brandi away, and "B" emerged. This is the part of me that would step up to ensure that I never got hurt again; in my mind, this was my bodyguard and the persona within me that would always make sure that I did not make a fool out of myself. "B" was there to say what Brandi wouldn't, and as crazy as I sound saying this right now, "she" was my balancer.

Regardless of alter egos, God's hand stayed on me. I'll never forget the one night my girls and I went downtown to a party for A&T Homecoming weekend. There I was in all black and my hair perfect. Little did we know that it would begin raining cats and dogs outside as we waited to get in. By the time we gained admission and went to the bathroom, all of my hard work was down the drain. There I was, trying to take my nails to readjust my hair to no avail. After a few attempts I had decided that was it, and it didn't matter since I would sweat it out on the dance floor anyway. Finally, we decided to leave, only to hear the sound of the rain sound like a tsunami instead. We stood under a canopy plotting our run-on Elm Street downtown. As we took off, we knew we had roughly three blocks to travel, but we were determined to make it there without getting wet. We got to the first stop sign. As we waited to cross (yes, still in the rain) a car with three men came up beside us. "Hey beautiful ladies, it's raining too hard for y'all to be out here like this," he said with a huge smile on his face. He then told us that he and his friends felt bad for us and were willing to give us a ride to our cars. I looked at my homegirl, she looked back and we shrugged simultaneously. The door flung open and without hesitation we jumped in. We had no idea who these men were, but we didn't care, we just wanted to get out of the rain. They were extremely quiet for those three blocks and did not ask many questions at all outside of where our car was. When we finally arrived, we thanked them and they drove off. My girl and I didn't discuss it then but a few years later she brought it up.

"Hey B, do you remember that night when we were running in the rain and those guys picked us up?"

"Of course, T! Why you bring that up?"

"Because I was just thinking – I don't think that we would have made it out of that situation if you had not been there. The only reason we made it out alive was because of you."

Time and experience solidified this statement. One night we were at Bentley's. There I was in one of my favorite outfits on Old School night. This was when the older, more seasoned crowd came through. As for me, I was there for the flirtation and the drinks; I had no intent on getting a sugar daddy, but instead just wanted some comedy relief. The club was kind of dead that night, but we were dressed for the occasion and paid our money so we had no intention on leaving. The music was going, and the club lights were flowing when I looked up and met eyes with this man across the room. He was dark, I mean like midnight. His eyes were deep-set and piercing. He stared then motioned for me to come over. There I was strutting with my model walk, ready to get at least a drink or two out of him.

"Hey," he said.

I smiled and replied back.

"Listen, I don't know who you are, but you need to leave."

My smile quickly faded as I stood confused and offended.

"I don't know where you're supposed to be, but it's not here. I need you to find where you are supposed to be and get there."

I tried to interject, but he continued,

"Why did you come with those girls?"

"They're my fri...."

"No, they aren't your friends. Don't say that. I know they aren't because when they walked in, my boys and I had already plotted what we would to do them. When you came in, I opened my mouth to spit my plan about you and my tongue went to the roof of my mouth. It didn't release until you walked over here. So yes, I need you to get where you're supposed to be, because you're messing up my high!"

I backed up, shocked, offended but most of all, regretting the stroll I took over there. In my mind,

I deserved to escape this "high interrupt" he spent so much time breaking down to me. I just wanted to escape — why could I not escape God, even in the crevices of the club life? Time progressed and I became more and more cold and sinister. I loved who I loved but foolishness was one thing that I did not do. Guys would approach me, some correctly, but for the most part, corny and completely, off target. They would approach me at the ATM with lines like,

"So, you got a 20 in there for me?"

I remember one night; this one guy caught me on a really bad night. I looked up, smiled, and said,

"Of course, I don't but since you live with your mom you should be good with the allowance, she gives you."

Now had the conversation just been between us it would have been less embarrassing, but since it happened in front of the bathrooms, of course he got the business right there and his friends did not allow him to live a moment of it down. In my opinion, every man was about to feel my rath, from my ex-fiancé', to my ex-husband and all of my rendezvous, it was my turn to show them who I had the capacity to really be.

No matter where I went, the oil on my life followed. There was a Reggae club downtown that I frequented; my homegirl couldn't stand Reggae music, but for me, it was my vibe. The music was everything and filled the space of all three floors of the club. After a much needed "dance hall" session, I went to the bathroom to freshen up. The door swung open and there stood a girl who was a friend of mine who we will call "Hailey"; we went to church together at the previous fellowship. She yelled my name and wasted no time going in on me.

"Brandi, I can't believe you!

How could you do that to your house?"

They took a step back, knowing that if I took a step up, they would have to remove me from the premises. Her accusations continued, proving that she had clearly picked a side concerning my separation and pending divorce. Alcohol had her voice on one thousand as she continued to hurl insults at me. Finally, I had reached my boiling point and before I knew it, blurted out,

"I ruined my house?! In that case why don't you go and ask him about...?"

Immediately all of the drunkenness left her veins. The same voice that told me how horrible I was now filled the atmosphere with apologies. In my heart I wanted to say no hard feelings and move forward, but the "B" in me would not allow it. Encounters such as these made me search out other places to spend my time. Sometimes, it was cool, but other times it landed me in troubling circumstances like when I was thrown into a bathroom and almost raped or when I picked up a modeling job only to be sexually assaulted and run out with barely a garment of clothing on.

These moments eventually led me to another club. This one was known for strippers, which I was never into, but nevertheless often gave me something to laugh at. It was here that an old obsession came to the forefront, my obsession with "bad boys." There was just something about them, and I had no idea that no one was watching me. I don't know how long his eyes were fixed on me, but definitely long enough to know that he wanted to see what was up with me. He wouldn't walk over, but stood up against the bar, dressed from head to toe, shades on, faint smile, and a stance that invited me into his space. One thing I had never been into was big boys, but this one was different; he had some kind of swag that pulled me into his atmosphere. He told me that he was into music and was just out that night looking for some down time. His approach was cool, different, not like the rest, and I was undeniably intrigued. Numbers were exchanged and within minutes we were on the phone. Within days, he had me driving to his city, about thirty minutes away from me to see him. More than anything I was excited to see him produce music. He had a friend named "Buzz," who had a studio built at the bottom of his parents' house. The first day I saw my guy get in the booth, I was head over heels. The flex in his voice and the way he put words together stirred me. Weight didn't matter; the fact that he had a dream vacuumed me into his world and from that moment I was committed to helping him shine.

Every day that I had off, I was right there with him. I would drop off my son at school and head to wherever he was. He didn't have a car, but I didn't care because he was pursuing a dream and I was there for it. We had to be no more than three weeks in when I got the call:

"Hey B! What are you doing right now?"

"Nothing! What's up?"

"Well, I have a situation I need your help with."

"What's that?"

"I just spoke with my attorney. Some crazy stuff has popped off and I have to go to jail."

Now let me be clear, we were only three weeks in but I had already faceted myself to him. Before he could ask for anything, I asked what I could do.

"Well, I just need about $800 to fix this."

Here I am a single parent who had to choose between lunchables and making spaghetti, trying to figure out a man's "bail out" who I had just met. For me, this was my moment to prove that I still had potential, despite what any previous relationship tried to tell me.

"I'm going to figure it out, bae.

You're not going to jail."

I went home and began looking through everything I had until it hit me — sell your wedding ring, your band, necklace, and watch. I had NEVER been in a pawn shop, but was so committed to the cause that I was determined to figure it out. I walked in and met eyes with a girl I went to high school with. My first response was embarrassment but she made me feel comfortable in no time. I didn't tell her why, but instead how much I needed; within an hour, I had it and was off to rescue my new Beau. I was such a fool.

I took him the money, feeling like a whole "bad boy's girl," and from that moment I became just that, "his" girl." In his eyes, because I came through for him on that, I could be trusted with more. For him, "more" was the ability to make deals with me in the car. It included crackheads coming up to my car windows asking for things that were totally oblivious to me. To this day I am still guessing the undercover cops knew I was thrown off by it too, as they would ride by my car in unmarked mini vans, make eye contact with me, nod their head, and keep driving. This new life of mine even included people rolling up on me being willing to get me whatever I needed, be it socks, toothpaste, whatever, they were at my command. I never understood where they got the items from – all I knew was that I said it and it showed up. I wasn't dumb then and I'm certainly not now, so let's just say I never asked and they never told.

To the community, I was the good girl who ended up with a bad boy. There was nothing about me that looked like I should have been dating him; I straight up stood out like a green thumb! The world saw the rough side of him, but I got to see the teddy bear in him and in many ways, became his balance, despite the other relationships he left with loose ends all around us. There were other girls, but I had become his main girl, you know, the one he would take out in public the most, and so I resolved to be good with that. Whatever I wanted, he made sure I got, whether food, time, just about anything, but not without consequence. When tax season would come, it would always show up with a monetary request and I would always come through. We would follow up by going to the mall, and the same money I just gave him, he would use to buy something for me. Because I was "down," it would then become my responsibility to amp him up and make him feel good for his "sacrifice" for me, even though the money he held and used was being done so by my own blood, sweat and tears.

Time progressed and love grew, until I finally caught wind that I had now become the side piece. DM's would show up in my social media accounts from girls I had never met but were claiming to have a relationship with him. There were a few times that he would let me ride with him, but contrary to my belief, the car was not even his. He had spots where he would conduct business; he was seen as a staple in the streets but over time to me, the guy I met in the club faded and the guy who stood before me was not even a close second to the first one presented. One day, while we were out, he began experiencing chest pain. Being the good girlfriend, I immediately rushed him to the hospital. I even left at one point to get my son and bring him back, since I was determined not to leave him alone. The diagnosis came, but I continued to focus on him. As he was resting, God's voice flooded my spirit,

"Can you imagine this being your life?

Always in the hospital because of him?"

I didn't even have to respond, God knew my answer. When it came time for him to be discharged, I helped him get packed up and head to the desk. As we approached I came face-to-face with someone I had not seen in years, my ex-fiancé's wife, who was the one he had cheated on me with years before, who was now a nurse. Our eyes met and though she tried to balance in on her professionalism, her eyes told a story that her mouth could not formulate, but I was surely hoping that she would try. There I was standing face to face with my past with just two questions in mind,

"Was it worth it? Do you feel better now?"

We completed the transaction and left. Regardless of the circumstance I now faced with my current, seeing the sadness of my past brought a sadistic joy that was borderline sickening. It was then that I learned that wallowing in someone else's pain and sorrow really means that you are painful and sorrowful yourself, as I looked at the one with whom I had become another number two, three or maybe even four.

Eventually, I used that truth to begin the demolition of our relationship, but as with most unhealthy obsessions, it didn't just "end" but was filled with more one-night cuddy buddy encounters, second and third chances, which all began with basic things like him needing a ride or just having a question about something. Every time I fell for it, he would have this huge grin afterwards as if to say, "I still got it, and I still got you, too." If he thought that, he was right, he kind of did, but he didn't know that at this point game peeped game so I had him, but also him, and him and him, too, and so for me having this dude this one night was more like ordering a kid's meal knowing I had access to whatever number I wanted later. I became his fall back and he became my play toy — just like that I went from "RockCitySouth's girl," to RockCitySouth done, but he would never know it, at least not yet.

GOD

7.

SUNDAY MORNING

My son was safe, so it didn't matter where I laid my head on the weekends. This weekend, I woke up on the bed with my "bad boy," at what I will safely call "the spot." The light came piercing through the window, letting me know that it was time to get up.

A few weeks before I had received a request from a local church to come dance. I had no desire to do so for obvious reasons, but the Elect Lady of the house insisted, so having no more fight in me, I agreed. There was no part of me that wanted to go, knowing that my lifestyle alone could get me electrocuted by the Lord, but I did not want to disappoint her, so I prepared to leave. I threw my dance vessel outfit on quickly, knelt down to kiss my guy, told him I would check in later and I was off. I had danced at this church years before, as they did not have a dance ministry, so I would go once a month to serve. Knowing that I felt as if I was well below accepted at the current ministry I attended, going there to dance made me feel as if I really was anointed and like God really used me, too. Since the last time I had come, though they did not know everything that had happened with me, they did know that my ex-husband and I were no longer together; in other crowds where that became the scarlet letter on my chest, they did not think another thing about it. Married or not, they wanted me to come so I showed up. I danced and God moved. It threw me how I could be into my "other life" so deep and God still see fit to use me, but I remained appreciative through the process. At the end of the service the altar call came. Being that I had not been in church since before my separation, I was determined to tip-toe out, but that wasn't in the plan. The music came on and everyone stood. The ministers took their place in the front, facing the congregation, eyes closed, hands extended. Eventually, the Elect Lady walked over to me and said....

"I'm not here to change your mind. I just want to let you know that God says He simply wants to make you whole."

The ugly cry commenced, as I got myself together and stumbled in that moment. Many thoughts flooded my mind, current ones, and flashbacks, too! How could God forgive me? How could He even still look at me the same? I had JUST left the hideout from sleeping with a man I was not married to hours before and now here I stood with a Word of grace before me as if God did not even know what I had done just moments earlier!

In that moment I did not care about the process of explaining to my new world how I made my way back to the God of everything who had never given up on me. Here this room of people stood, having seen me at some of my best moments, now witnessing one of the lowest points of my life. There I was, having danced before the people so powerfully that people began to shout, cry, and praise the Lord; now they would see those same shouts and tears become my own. I do not know how, maybe someone walked with me, but I made my way to the front and gave my heart back to the Lord and became a member of that church the same day.

It was in this moment that I began to understand the grace that was really on my life and the truth that God truly kept me, even when I was on the street. The church I had joined was more intimate in size, but that did not matter. In fact, I believe that part of me desired that more, anyway. Joy took over me as I considered how, being that this church was in a different city, I would not have to be worried about ducking or dodging from the church I had been forced to leave. I would no longer have to go to a different Wal-Mart because of the stares from the former church members I would receive at the one they would always post up at after church was over. Despite the small town feeling that I had just connected myself too, it felt more peaceful there. I was not worried about the drive or the distance, I was just happy to be somewhere, a place where God still loved me and it seemed like the people did, too.

It did not take long before they were trying to put me to work and trust, despite the processes I was still going through, I was ready. Truthfully, I believe I just wanted to just get back to where I was in ministry where it all made sense. I already knew that by default I would be on the dance ministry, but anywhere they wanted me I was willing to be because, well, regardless of the church or the club, I had always been a servant. Sure, probably a year and a half had passed by this point of this new life I had embraced going back into the world, but in one fleeting moment and decision all of that changed, or did it?

8.

BETWEEN YES AND MAYBE

Let me keep it H.O.T. with you for a moment. (For those that don't know, H.O.T. is "Honest," "Open," and "Transparent." Shout out to #TeamTisdale, shameless plug!) When one gives their heart to God, whether for the first time one millionth time, there is a refreshing that happens internally, however the world doesn't get the memo and I would even venture to say that your flesh doesn't either. For me, just because I said yes, that didn't mean that I was done, and my actions proved just that.

Despite confessing that I was done with "bad boy" or even the club, that proved to be a lie. Instead, I had convinced myself that I could do and have both. For me, I had built a loyalty with those in the world, after all, they were the ones who were there for me when the church, in my view, turned their backs. When I was totally holy and sanctified, they were there without a hitch, but when all hell broke loose my deliverance was bound by chains put on by the very same place that had served as my safe haven for years. So yes, I had moved on and yes, I had joined this new church, but no, my other life was not out of my bloodstream yet.

"Hey B, you coming out tonight?"

"Yea babe, I'll meet you there."

How could I ever tell her "no"? After all, she had become my best friend and had walked with me through the worst place of my life. She freed me up and let me know that it was okay to be "B" without apologies. 10:00pm came and like clockwork I would go change my clothes and watch for 11:00pm to hit so I could log out and go meet my people. Those nights, it didn't matter to me who I danced with — I had said yes but baby, I was I still running.

I remember one night being at Bentley's until the club closed for the evening. That for us was not unusual but what was different for me was a boldness that I had never executed. That night, I danced with someone I had never seen before. He was tall, handsome, hair cornrowed back, flashy smile, dimples, kind of a Master P swag. He seemed fairly mesmerized by me and Lord knows I was by him, too. By the end of the night, I had decided that I was going to get his number at the very least. As dark as that room was I saw him as he left, taking one last glance back at me. I yelled,

"Hey I see you! What's your number? Shout it!"

Just as soon as I said it, he smiled and blurted it out as his girl cousins shoved him out of the door. I was twisted that night but my memory was on point. The next morning, the very first thing that I thought when I woke up was,

"Text that dude. 336...."

So, I did. Family, I didn't even know his name. So here I go, boldness continued. The conversation went something like this.

"Hey. I hope this is you. Were you at Bentley's last night?"

He responded,

"Yea. You're "her!"

I smiled. I can't say if it was because he remembered me or because I no longer had to feel embarrassed about not knowing his name, because he didn't know mine either. Before the exchange was over, names were made clear too, but for the purposes of this story I will simply call him, "T."

He was a complete gentleman despite his thug appearance if you will. Believe it or not, he worked at a funeral home; that seemed a little morbid to me, but it was "him" so I bypassed that little fact; I mean at least he had a job! He was a single parent like me and was the father to a beautiful little girl who I got to meet at least once, which was new for me considering the last relationships that had kids kept me a secret for the most part. We would meet up for lunch and talk all the time. Church conversations came up but I didn't feel the need to talk about my most recent decisions because I was still working double duty if you will. We both had hurts but somehow and someway, found a way to let each other in. We had not applied titles because of that very thing, the hurt, but we also knew how much we were feeling each other, too.

One night, he came by my apartment. We hung out, watched TV, and talked but eventually that night turned into something else. It was not like the experiences of the others, knowing that I was one of many, but this time it felt like I was the only one. The moment commenced and I, well, I knew he was fully present but had resolved that I could not be, knowing that being dropped again simply could not be my lot.

After the deed was done, quietness settled over the room. I looked over. He had sat up by now, with his hands covering his face. I looked for a moment thinking that maybe he was just getting himself together, until I heard sniffing, then what sounded like crying. I reached for him, asked him what was wrong and this is what he said.....

"We should have never done this. I should have never allowed it. I should have never allowed you to slip – you're a woman of God."

I stopped, because though we had previous conversations about faith, I really did not go into the depth of how much I was committed to God years before. He continued to repeat his words,

"B, this isn't right. You're a woman of God. I should have stopped it; I should have never let you slip. You are absolutely beautiful; I should have stopped. I am so sorry."

I couldn't even cry because shock had stolen every tear. There I stood, now, eye to eye with him, apologizing too, thinking that God would keep my YES secret, but instead, He shared it with one that I would tell eventually but didn't want tell just yet; it simply would have been too much red tape to explain. It was not long after that moment that T reached out saying that we could no longer see each other, that he was still hurt by his daughter's mother and did not want to bring me into that. I understood, and yes, I was upset all at the same time. Yes I had a whole player mentality when I engaged with men, but that wasn't really me at all. Though I would be completely nonchalant, I still believed in love and possibilities and would often write my name with their last name tagged on the back end just to see how it would look. This time I thought that maybe this one could have been the "wright" one, but the hurt we had both endured would not allow it.

As weird as it sounds, just as quickly as "the wright one" appeared in my life, he disappeared, and I was back to my old rhythm if you will. Somehow and some way I had figured out how to be present at the club all weekend while still being a church and every place they needed me to occupy as well. I was still drinking and laying down, though not as much, yet just enough to let my flesh know that I was still there for it. As usual, it also was not unusual to wake up fully clothed from the night before, and this one morning I recall was no different. A pink strapless dress and silver stiletto heels graced my bed as the makeup from the night before smeared my pillowcase. As had always been the case since my youth, I did not have a hangover this morning either, but my room felt especially bright. When I would have normally been able to shower myself into sobriety and make it to church, that morning I found it to be impossible. I tossed and turned and even wondered why the blinds on my window weren't doing their job. As I fussed in my mind, a voice I had not heard in well over a year began booming in my ear:

"ARE YOU DONE YET?

ARE YOU DONE BEING GOD?"

I tossed again because SURELY Holy Spirit has not come in my apartment with me, looking like this, in this condition, right now, right? (Sidenote, yes you guessed it! I had rededicated but still had not heard the voice of God concerning my life, until now.)

"ARE YOU DONE BEING GOD?

CAN I BE GOD NOW?

CAN I BE YOUR GOD TODAY?"

I laid there, tears streaming as I lay on my back, still fully clothed. There was no room to plead my case. In this moment it did not matter what I felt that my ex-husband had done to me, what the church had done to me or anyone else; in this moment it was all about what I had done to myself, who I had allowed myself to become and who I had restricted God to be for me.

"Yes Lord, Yes."

I don't know how loud I said it, but it felt like I was screaming as far as my spirit was concerned. I don't know how many times I said it but I knew that my soul meant it and that I was tired of running.

"GOOD. I'M GOING TO ASK YOU THIS QUESTION EVERY DAY. I WILL ASK YOU UNTIL YOU'RE SO CONSISTENT THAT I DON'T HAVE TO ASK YOU ANYMORE."

And then, the booming voice left. Just like that. As quickly as He had come, He was gone and believe it or not, my flesh was afraid of the YES but my spirit was grateful for His intervention. This would be marked as the first of many.

It seemed as if the church world did not get word of my dance "retirement," by way of church hurt, divorce, and destruction. One request came by way of a Pastor who I worked with. Based on my nightly routine, I thought that she would know my position without asking, but even if she did, this did not stop her request. She had heard about my dance ministry and was determined to have me come minister, at the beach. I had never ministered so far away and counted it an honor to do so. My goddaughter and I arrived with nothing more than a tank of gas and a few dollars to my name. I had to pay for our room which I charged to a card that had every right to decline but went through against my account. We ministered with power, and many were blessed, but nothing prepared me for what would happen that evening, the ashes.

The Pastor brought us together on the beach and told us that there were things holding us back that we had to release. Women began weeping and agreeing; I agreed but refused to weep. Despite dance, rage had become my friend and I had no intention of letting it go. She gave us sticky notes and told us to write down what was holding me back. On my paper I wrote one word....

R.O.B.

My ex-husband's name.

My insecurity, the church hurt, my doubt or fear did not make the list, only his name. In my view, had he not happened I would not have gone through what I went through, it was all his fault. I balled up my paper and threw it in the fire pit they had prepared. They applied sand to make the fire go out, took the remains, and had us put them in tiny glass bottles with a cork. The next instructions came,

"One by one, you all will walk up that pier and toss your bottle into the ocean as a prophetic sign that you are letting go."

Everyone did as instructed, and finally, it was my turn. There I was, short hair, in my long purple and white maxi-dress, preparing for what felt like the walk of doom. All I could think about was how my releasing him meant that he would get away with the hurt applied to my life. My releasing him meant that he would escape the repercussions of what I felt he had done to me. I couldn't let him get away with that, I just couldn't. As I walked, the breeze became stronger, as people were fishing off the very pier I walked up, looking completely unbothered. The more I walked, the more the wind blew until,

"Brandi. Brandi, do you hear me? Do you hear me because I hear you."

I knew exactly Who that was, not my imagination or the wind, it was Holy Spirit.

"Can you feel Me? I feel you."

I continued to walk, as I wondered if those fishing could hear what I heard, but obviously that was a no-go. I reached the edge of the pier, and as an act of not faith, but simply to be a team player I prepared to toss the bottle, and then,

"Call him and let him know you release him."

I couldn't, I couldn't do it. I didn't feel like I could do it, and God knew that, too.

"If You are God, and You are everywhere, why can't You tell him for me?"

I thank God that He really knows me, because He could have smote me for that one.

"Let him know you release him."

With my phone in my other hand, I tried, then found myself texting, "Hey Rob. I just want to let you know that I forgive and release you. I'm not holding on to you anymore, you are free." His reply back sounded like exactly what he would say, "Are you trying to kill me," to which I quickly replied, "No, I'm not," with a smiley face. I responded, genuinely smiled, and then I threw my bottle in the ocean and returned safely to the seashore.

9.

WHEN PARALYSIS BIRTHS YES

Being hard-headed is something else, but so is testing God's grace on your life, too. Now, one would think that when God rolls up in your room while you still have on your clothes from the party the night before and promises you His backing, that you would get what the seasoned would call, some "act right," but instead I was acting, "all wrong." Now don't hear what I'm not saying, that encounter scared the living daylights out of me, but it did not completely arrest the behaviors in me. I was still going to the club, but not as much. I would still drink, but not as potent. I would still lay down, but just be more selective and spaced out. In my mind, my adjustments were enough because after all, less than two years before, my life had completely been ripped away from me and plus, I still had a point to prove to my ex-husband, right?

As God promised though, every day He came with the same question and I came with the same answer. Day by day I broke the same YES I gave Him. Every morning I gave Him another and He accepted it knowing that within hours it would be broken again,

119

so I guess He decided to tamper with my desire. I went from going to the club every weekend to every weekend but only one night. I went from dropping everything at the right word to lay down with someone I knew could have cared less about me as a person, to declining calls and going ghost on some. It wasn't until I found myself in this place that I realized how crazy I felt and probably looked. I began counting up how much I had spent on dresses, nails, hair, lashes, pedicures and the list went on. The thought of wearing different outfits for the same people every weekend dancing to the same music made me sick to my stomach; hundreds of dollars every week was squandered on something that pacified my pain but was slowly and surely destroying my life.

So, just like that I stopped, but life caught up to me. Deja vu is a dangerous drug of choice, as cramping and throwing up commenced. It could not be, it just couldn't. Last time I knew exactly who, but this time, I had no clue. Confirmation came back, tears shed and there I was, pregnant, again. The embarrassment overflowed within because, well, I was on the up and up or so I thought. I decided to quit what I was doing but did so too late. The father was one of three, and though I didn't know who, I also knew that they didn't care, as that was not the nature of our relationship. As with the first of my youth, I resolved to do the same, but this time, bear the burden alone. I drove up to the place, this time closer than the first, with a hoodie covering my head and shades in hopes that no one would recognize me. I sat in the waiting room, this time at a different location but similar, since I had met one of my girls there once to console her concerning what she had done, too. I got my money together, even with it being the last of what I had in that moment, to do what I swore I would never do again, have another abortion. This time, I needed help, I needed sedation.

As they administered it they promised me that everything would be alright, much like the first. I remember looking up and seeing the cloud wallpaper they had applied, the same wallpaper the nurse told me to focus on with consolations of, "That's where your baby is. They know you love them. They understand." I tried to believe it, but I didn't even understand and I knew that God didn't either. After it was over and I was permitted to leave, I was greeted at the end of the parking lot by those holding signs. Their looks of discouragement and condemnation overwhelmed me, but I couldn't let them see me cry; instead I decided to weep in the comfort of my own space as I processed the reality of what I had done.

When I would be captivated into believing that this was the worse challenge that I could overcome, I would find that to be completely untrue. As had been the case before, despite the things that I had done, God still somehow and some way, used me for His glory. I know what you are about to say,

29 For the gifts and the calling of God are irrevocable [for He does not withdraw what He has given, nor does He change His mind about those to whom He gives His grace or to whom He sends His call].

Romans 11:29

While this Word remains true, it is amazing how we as believers or His redeemed can feel as if we are disqualified from the very Word that showers over us daily. In life I had been paralyzed in so many ways, my mind, heart, soul, money, but nothing would prepare me for the paralysis of my own body.

There I was on a Sunday morning doing God's will for my life. We had practiced for weeks for this one song, "I Choose to Worship," by Wes Morgan. I was ready. I even remember us praying over the music and how the people would receive what God desired to present to His people that day. I had just reconnected with a friend who I had not seen in years, a man, who like me had been through some really similar places and at the time, also like me, was working to recover from it all. We had messaged simply that day that we hoped one another had a great service. It was nothing major, just a message.

The song came on and we began to dance. Every movement was engulfed by the presence of God; it was completely undeniable. We stood as three but moved as one, and we knew that God was in the midst. As we worshiped, I made a move, one move that changed the trajectory of everything. I turned, I kicked, nothing high but just enough and then it happened. I felt my knee cap swivel from the front of my leg to the back and then back to the front. Fire began to run up and down my leg. I wanted to scream, but the worship happening had to go on and I dared not interrupt it, so I slowly slid to the floor in perfect dancer posture so much so that the other congregants thought that God had taken me up and worship. They praised and I laid, wondering what had just happened to me but following the song....

"He's healing me, I'm gonna worship..."

Tears fell down the sides of my face into my ears as I laid there wondering when someone would pick me up in the spirit? There I was on the floor with dancers looking still but only for a moment as I lifted my hands and released a signal for them to keep dancing. The song finally concluded, and in my mind, I would just get up with minor assistance and be fine, but as I sat up and attempted to move I realized that I couldn't. Two men from the church rushed to my aid and walked me to the office. The walk that should have felt like thirty seconds felt like hours, as they took my in my Elect Lady's office and sat me down.

There I sat in that room with the yellow walls, tears streaming and confusion looming. As service progressed I kept thanking God, but the inside of my soul was beyond afraid. Among the questions, there was the one that had me wondering how I would drive home, or how would my son respond to this? How would I get to work? I just needed someone, anyone to calm me down.

So, I called "him." No we weren't together but I called, hoping that I would not catch him in the middle of his Adjutant duties but feeling as if I needed to hear his voice. We had met briefly in high school at our senior prom only saying hello, only to be reintroduced in the midst of all of this captivity and drama. My plan upon first re-introduction after the loss of a mutual friend some time before, was to, for lack of better terms "turn him out," but God quickly put me in my place when He told me that if I wanted this one, I would be the one who would have to come up.

His look, beautiful, he soul, intriguing, and needless to say God knew that I was scoping him out. I liked him but, in this moment, I just needed him to tell me that everything would be okay which was way more than he was obligated to do for me. His response was sweet and melodic, almost as if he was ready to convey just what I needed. Little did I know that I would later find out that when I called, he was sitting in the pulpit but saw me calling and knew that he needed to pick up the phone. He answered, I updated, and he immediately began to pray. After telling me to contact him once I got home, I wiped my face, agreed, and prepared to find a way to get myself up.

What I could do without effort just hours before had just become an unruly task, as I tried to shift my weight from my left leg to my right in hopes of at least limping to my car. For every try, fear overwhelmed me, as I realized that weight on my left leg at all was not an option, so I stepped on my right and pulled my left behind me. I finally made it into the hallway, crying more now than ever. As I leaned my body against the wall, I did so determined to make it to my car. When I was about halfway there, the same two young men that helped me up were running to me, offering to help me walk while grabbing the keys to bring my car closer to the building. This assistance came unexpected, as I was mentally preparing to reenact the Kill Bill movie scene where a character fresh out of a coma, took a chance to drag her own body to freedom.

Down the road I drove, still in my dance garments, tears rolling while driving with my good leg. Twenty-two minutes led me to my apartment complex with one question in mind: If I couldn't get out of the church on one level and into my car without moving like a paralytic, how would I make it the second level of my apartment? I drove up, parked, and contemplated. After a while, I devised a plan and opened my car door. My garments dragged across the ground as I stepped on my right and pulled my left leg from behind. As I approached the stairway it had become clear that I would need to use the rails as crutches of sorts, and so I did just that. I had never been through an injury like this, much less a dance injury, but I promise you that God was leading every one of my movements. As I went up the stairs one by one, memories flashed of the song my oldest goddaughter, Keyona, and I danced to, "I Trust You," by Anthony Brown.

We ministered this song well before all hell began breaking loose. In one part of the song I fell to the floor, but when the major chorus came up, I began army crawling across the floor in desperation of getting to my Father. I took one step at a time, and once I reached the top, took a sigh of relief. Step, drag, step, drag, became the pattern until I got in the door. Plopping on the couch, I took a moment to try and figure out how to proceed. I called into work and let my ex-husband know that he could bring him by. It didn't take long before the door knocked and I yelled for them to give me some time. Getting up was a task and that seemed to get more difficult by the moment, but according to my determination, this was temporal and would be fine morning. My ex asked questions, and my son did, too; after a while he left, and there we were, just my son and I.

The next morning showed up, and despite my biggest expectations, nothing was any better concerning my condition but in fact it was now swollen to the high heavens! As I woke my baby boy up, I realized that I would not be able to walk him to the bus stop; he was only five years old. I got him ready and prayed as I did so,

"God I can't walk down the stairs. God protect my baby, PLEASE."

I remember getting him out the door with our next door neighbor who was the same age and attended the same school. I hopped to his room and looked out the window as I watched for their school bus. I knew that God forbid something tried to happen, that I would not make it down there in time, so every moment I watched was contained with more prayers that his bus would just go ahead and show up! I went on like this for three days – call into work, get my son off to school, go sit back down, wait for him to get out, until the third day came and I knew that I had to do something. My leg was not getting any better and I knew that the only way to reverse whatever had occurred was to get help. I drove to the nearest, and most recommended urgent care. I parked my car, pulled myself out and began walking and dragging towards the building. Two nurses rushed out with a wheelchair,

"Ma'am what are you doing!?!"

I calmly explained why I was there as they put me in the wheelchair and began to push me inside. I waited in the patient room, ready to get a prescription, maybe some time off work and walk out, but instead I got this:

"Brandi, bend your knee for me. Brandi, did you hear me...bend your knee. Matter of fact, flex your foot."

Pain surged through my body as I did all I could for the physician's review. He stopped me and told me that nothing was moving, but my pain level told me otherwise. Before I left that day I received the following news,

"Brandi, you have sustained a major injury to your knee. To be honest, I would not recommend

you dancing again. For lack of better terms, your leg is paralyzed, and will not be otherwise until it decides to respond to therapy."

PARALYZED? How? What?

I was ready for my note for a few days off, but not paralysis. When I left that day, I left with a referral, knee brace and leg immobilizer, and thus began my journey of recovering from just that, paralysis.

The next weeks were filled with disability paperwork, missed wages, and yes, physical therapy. My practitioner was mean as a rattlesnake and I could not, for the life of me, figure out why she was still working there. After my doctor cleared me of any tearing needing surgery, therapy began until I made it stop. Her teachings were cool, but her attitude was all the fuel I needed to stop. This refusal gave me a lot more time at my apartment, which led to a whole lot more time with the Lord. One of the worst things I could have done during those few days was to take a mirror and look at the back of my leg. It was completely black and blue all across the back and nearly made me throw up. Anger filled my soul as I contemplated how God could allow me to dance on slippery floors in five inch heels without injury but allow me to shift to a place of immobility all because I was obedient in dancing for Him. Needless to say, life was not adding up, at all. Day in and day out I sat, waiting for a healing until finally I could not hold anymore,

"Lord heal me."

Silence filled the room.

"Lord, heal me!"

This time I added on force.

"Will you preach my gospel?"

"Wait Lord, what are you talking about? I just need you to heal me!"

"Will you do what I said?"

"But God!"

"if you won't preach say no, so that I can get the one who will."

"All I want is for you to heal me!"

"Will....you....preach...or....not?"

He didn't say anything less and He didn't say anything more. As I had said just a few rooms away months ago, another YES filled my mouth, but this time

131

I knew that there was no wiggle room or even time to digress; this time it was all or nothing. I sat in that moment, looking at my leg. It was black and blue when I asked God to heal me and remained black and blue when I gave God my YES. Let me break from my story and share this truth with you — we can never give God a YES with wrong motives. The "Brandi" in me was hoping that maybe the seriousness of my answer would have removed the swelling, restored color and mobility too all in one moment, but that did not happen. Saying YES did not remove the paralysis that I faced, and yet God was downloading instructions to me as if what I was going through did not even exist.

Sunday came before I knew it, and it was time for me to do what God instructed. I stumbled around all morning looking for the easiest outfit to throw on. Holy Spirit said I had to go to church and have a conversation with my Pastor, and regardless of my condition, nothing could stop that meeting. Once I got in the car the rest was a piece of cake considering that my injury did not affect my driving leg. I got there, maneuvered myself out of the car and made my way to the sanctuary. Since many had not seen or spoke with me during the week, my arrival held a bit of shock as they saw me hobble in. I grabbed a seat near the windows, not my usual place, but closest to the door. As my Pastor entered in, he paused for a moment, put his hand on my knee and prayed. Tears fell as I felt every Word and agreed. Church that day was amazing; once it was done, I knew that I had to speak with him. I waited my turn and even made sure that I went last, knowing that this conversation would not be like the ones that preceded me. As I entered his office, my flesh was all over the place but my spirit remained sound. "Bishop, can we talk," I asked as I spoke into the door slightly cracked. "Of course, daughter," he responded, "come in." I must say that this meeting felt different, maybe since my father's passing took opportunities like this away from me, at least in my view. As I began to gather my words, they just pushed through in a way that I never expected.

"Bishop, I have a call on my life to preach the gospel, and..."

As I continued to speak, a smile came on his face. He began flipping through a calendar that sat on his desk as I continued. I told him about the open confession when I was eighteen years old and what happened on the couch at my apartment just days before. He smiled again, but this time, took the calendar and turned it around towards me.

"Yes, I know. I was just waiting on you."

I don't know if I can describe that moment as relief or borderline fear. For me, the most I had done when it came to preaching was the Youth Sunday services years before and the messages I preached on my karaoke machine, and now God was calling me beyond dance into the ministry of verbal display. He continued, "So let's pick a date for your initial sermon." Now keep in mind, I was FRESH out of the club, and thus figured that the best date for me was at least a year out, until he selected a date three months away. Despite the voices in my head that told me I was completely tripping, I agreed and February 27, 2011 became my initial sermon date.

Preparation did not just include the Word itself, but also my continued recovery. When I had attended physical therapy, I told them that I had two desires — to wear my heels again and be able to dance, and those desires had not changed but this time, preaching my initial sermon FREE of paralysis was added to my list. I had watched my physical therapy plan long enough to have a handle on what

I had to do to walk freely again, and decided that I would pursue that goal on my own at the gym instead. Every step of my recovery was led by God – I spent a lot of time on the stationary bicycles followed up with taking steps in the pool. For me, the pool was life, as it enabled me to do things with my leg that seemed impossible on "dry land." For weeks I went to the gym daily, determined to walk regardless of the prognosis I was given. When I wasn't at the gym, I was at home wrapping my right leg around my left, determined to make it bend. The more I tried the more painful it became, but I knew that this recovery would not come without it.

I can't say what drove me to determination this one day – maybe it was the push to recover or the irritation of trying to ride a bike, right side normally, but left leg requiring almost an unnatural levitation off the chair, but that day was it. I was tired of being handicapped and tired of being slowed down, so I decided to do something about it. I got off of the bicycle and made my way to a grass turf area nearby. This section of the gym looked like a football field, equipped with mats and some dumbbells, too. Among the equipment, was two bars that had been cemented in the ground, which reminded me of the ballet bars that I used in school. I grabbed the handle and slid myself down to the floor. Yes, I wondered how I would get back up, but first, I had to fix what was broken, me. I laid on my back just like I did at home, mentally preparing myself for what was to come. I wrapped my right leg around my left and forced my left knee to bend. The pain was indescribable but determination led the mission. I counted to five.

Then I released my hold.

Then, I did it again.

Have you ever been in so much pain that you could not cry? If so, that was me, but I kept repeating the process. After about the fourth pull there was a loud, audible pop and what sounded like a balloon deflating. I screamed. People including staff rushed over to help me up. I screamed again but this time, while declining help. I explained that this process required that I get myself up off the floor. They stepped back in both amazement and concern as I shifted myself from the floor to the bar and up on my feet. The same heat I felt at the time of my injury filled my leg again, but this time with movement. My muscles were so much in shock that they had no control but movement indeed. I could even point my toes! Victory filled my soul as my dream had become reality...that God one day would free me from the prognosis of never walking normally, and though I had not tried it yet, dancing too. Just as I called "him" when the injury took place, I called "him" about the recovery, too. Just as I had called him before I had no idea why I was doing it but knew that I just needed to hear whatever would flow from his lips to my ears.

"He" didn't live here, but instead was in South Carolina. From the moment of the onset of my injury, he showed up. Being in full-time ministry was not a lucrative move as you may be able to imagine, so he would often sell plasma just to fill his tank, come to North Carolina, check on me and take out my trash. This act of service went on for months, even as healing became my reality. As I was building strength, he helped me build what would be known as my first sermon, "The Diamond Aftermath." He was highly educated, both academically and theologically, but never allowed that to intimidate me. Oftentimes he would refer to me as a "jackleg preacher," as he counted down the days until I would become legitimate.

February came faster than a speeding bullet. There I was, with a black two-piece suit that my mother had purchased for me along with some of the baddest shoes I had ever worn. My hair was laid and my spirit was ready, as I had spent months preparing the perfect sermon. I sat there in the sanctuary, free of paralysis and grateful. The service on that Sunday morning began. Even as people flooded the room, sorrow flooded my soul as I longed for the presence of my father. Just as I was about to sink in my own tears, my Bishop came over to me, grabbed my hand, and walked me to the podium. I looked scanned the room, realizing that this was the moment that my life would change forever, as God was birthing a Word in me that would describe the next years of ministry, prophetically released from my mouth into the atmosphere.

7 But we have this *precious* treasure [the good news about salvation] in [unworthy] earthen vessels [of human frailty], so that the grandeur *and* surpassing greatness of the power will be [shown to be] from God [His sufficiency] and not from ourselves. 8 We are pressured in every way [hedged in], but not crushed; perplexed [unsure of finding a way out],

but not driven to despair; [9] hunted down and persecuted, but not deserted [to stand alone]; struck down, but never destroyed [10] always carrying around in the body the dying of Jesus, so that the [resurrection] life of Jesus also may be shown in our body.

2 Corinthians 4:7-10

In a flash, all I had written had been released as praise and worship filled the house. I took a deep breath, being glad that it was over. My Bishop came up to the podium, and as he would often say,

"Did our hearts not burn?"

I sat in disbelief of what had just occurred. Before I could even process it, he called me up and in his hands held my Certificate of License. I had been so focused on the sermon, I had not even considered the certificate, so needless to say, I wept like a baby. It was official, I was no longer a jack-leg, but instead now full-fledged.

10.

BLACK BALLED A-GAIN

Over the next couple of months, God began removing the appetite from my spirit of things I would have leaned on, from the club to men, too. Ones that normally could get me to "show up" in an instant no longer held my interest and they knew it. One night, Mr. RCS came by with his homeboy and pizza. When I opened the door, I already knew that he was waiting for me to be up on him, but every desire had left. As I opened the door, I could tell that he had already put his boy on, telling him that I used to be his main one who would never tell him no. He walked in like a "G" with his homeboy who had two boxes of Domino's pizza in hand. He told me that he was stopping through because he had a show to do at a local club, and as a result, could not think of a person he would rather see than me. As is current day, even then my face was unsaved — if you wanted to know what I was thinking, all you had to do was look at my face, and this night was no different. I can hear him now.....

"B, you 'gon do me like that?"

My face replied back without saying a word, "yea, yea I am." Needless to say, his homeboy chuckled as Mr. RCS picked his face up off my floor and prepared to leave. I had no idea, but it would be years before I heard from him again for reasons that I would have never imagined. By the time I heard back from him, it would be to apologize for every bad thing he had ever done to me in light of what he was currently experiencing in life. I can't tell you how many times I forgave him; I pray that he finally realized that I meant it.

Just as he rolled through, Mr. J did too, but this time by phone and more than anything wanting to know why I didn't tell him that I was going to end up preaching. His messages sounded distressed, as if he had a right to know and had been betrayed. I remember responding back plainly,

"Because I didn't think it mattered to you."

There was no reply. This day also served as our last conversation. Time went on, and God continued to remove what could not stay, people, places and yes things, too. I knew who I could remain connected to beyond my new decision, and my girl Tasha was one who God allowed. Though I had released the club scene, if she needed me, she knew where to find me and knew that would be there in an instant. When her birthday came up, I still went to the party even though it was at the club, well Shooters, anyway. As I arrived, people looked shocked to see me as they varied from, "Oh, sh**, hey B," to "Ummm, God bless you?" I would often laugh and say that just saying hello would do.

It was in these moments that God proved to me that I was done, and that He also showed people His love. I didn't come in bashing bibles on peoples' heads, nor did I come in conforming to what they were doing, but instead, but continued to be me, the new me, without apology yet still loving on my people. All the while, "he" was still there. Now let me be clear, we were not together but knew that we would eventually end up that way. December 2011 came and without a second thought, the day came when we knew that it would be him and I forever. He had watched me go through some of the roughest places of my life, and after watching him do the same, we knew that we could conquer the world together.

As I approached my first year as a minister, my Bishop advised me that it was time for the next step, to become an ordained Elder. The news came as a shock to me, but I was submitted and ready, so I accepted. One day I was at work and received word that I could get off early. Joy filled my soul as I thought about getting my son and spending some much needed quality time with him. As I was packing up, Holy Spirit made it really clear that this Thursday night would not be a chill night for me, but instead an evening of confrontation. His instructions were clear:

"Go to the place that hurt you and make things right. You can't accept Elder until you do it."

I didn't want to go. There was nothing in me that wanted to go. This place that had embraced me for years and spit me out, regardless of my transformation, in my mind did not deserve a chance to get anything right. When I needed them most, the majority had turned from me as if I was a bad habit, a cursed soul who left with no justification. There was a remnant that showed up periodically, but for the most part, only God came to where I was to pull me out. No matter how much I tried to strengthen my decision of disobedience, Holy Spirit kept the burden on my heart until I got my son, bought him a Happy Meal, and made my way to the church. As expected, many were surprised to see me, as it had been over a year since I had even stepped foot on the grounds.

144

Some knew about my ministry licensure while others were still reeling off of the lies that their text messages, meetings, and social media posts had produced.

"Brandi, oh yea, she's a crackhead now."

"Brandi, oh yea, I heard she's gay, too."

"Brandi, honey that girl is a straight up prostitute."

Oh, and the one that really got me,

"Brandi, such a sad story, I heard that she died. She should have just stayed instead of leaving like she did. I hope her son is okay."

So, you can imagine how the greeters looked when I walked up to the door. As irony would have it, do you remember the one I shared with you before who walked around my dance studio, only to touch the walls, laugh and leave? Well, this night it was her turn to greet. As I approached the door, her huge and welcoming smile immediately faded, as I walked in strong, confident, and somewhat recovered. Her eyes rolled so horrendously that I wanted to warn her as I would hear my mom say, that if she kept doing that eventually they would be stuck like that. She couldn't even say "hello," or "welcome," but instead grunted. God had removed a lot from me, but sarcasm was not one of them as I smiled bigger than the smile she originally produced and said,

"Hey A! It's so good to see you!"

Can you forgive my shadiness? Thank you! We walked beyond her and past the double doors and took our seat in the sanctuary. It was not long before my now, former Pastor and first spiritual father walked through the door. I had not heard much since I had been gone, but as he entered, I knew that something wasn't right. There he was, pressing but with assistance, while proceeding to the podium to deliver the bible study for that evening. I held back my tears, as I watched him press while considering what I allowed to remove me.

It wasn't him, it was the people.

It wasn't church hurt, it was people hurt.

Cameras continued to film as he scanned the room, paused, and said, "Is this even _____ anymore." One person responded with a weak cheer; he dropped his head, shaking it slowly as he continued. Within a few minutes, he concluded, and returned out of the same door that he had entered. Some people

146

came up to speak afterwards, but most just stared in disgust. Had I allowed their looks to drive me, I would have easily forgotten the reason why I was there, but Holy Spirit kept the mission in front of me.

The conversation with my first spiritual father did not take place that night or any night for that matter, but instead, through a letter, which included my repentance and a copy of my initial sermon CD. I told him I was sorry for leaving, and that despite the path I walked, God came back for me. I did not share what the people did — in my view none of that mattered, both in light of God's redemption and what his body enduring. I put the letter and CD in a manilla envelope, addressed it to him and on the back wrote, "No one is to open this except _____. Please do not send this through the loopholes, this is for him ONLY." Black magic marker filled the room as I made my point clear and dropped it in the mail.

With a new relationship in my grasp, and redemption in progress, the truth that even people in church challenged us on for over a year became our reality, as "we" became a couple. We were dating by the end of December 2011 and by this time engaged and married on June 9, 2012. "He" became Husband; his name is Omar, God's manifested love for me in the earth. Life for us literally hit the ground running. Time was swiftly approaching, and needless to say God's instruction was still ringing in my ear, ordination was coming, but I could not say YES until I knew that all was clear and well with my spiritual father. Two weeks into our marriage, we used a Sunday evening to go out to eat. As we arrived, I ran into my spiritual father's wife who greeted me with a big smile and a hug, too. She talked about how beautiful I looked at my wedding which shocked me because I didn't realize she was on social media like that. She then followed up with these words,

"He got your letter and listened to your CD.

He said he is so proud of you."

I stood, stunned, knowing that God used this innocent moment to affirm, release, and bless me all in the same breath. I knew then that what I needed had been confirmed. At the end of that month, I was ordained as Elder in the Lord's church, and the week after, confirmed that I was pregnant with our daughter, who had been conceived on our wedding night. I'm so glad I ran into my first spiritual father's wife that day; it was more than the release, it was the affirmation from his lips to my ears before he took his last breath.

I guess news of my redemption spread like wildfire, as I began hearing from some people I had not seen in some time; one individual, Bri, was one of them. She, like many of the others I was beginning to reconnect with, also went to church with me. I remember the awe I sat in, when she reached out to let me know that she was launching out in a vision that set the stage for the deliverance of women, and wanted me to be a part of the team. Without a second thought I gladly accepted; it was then she shared with me the conditions. Within the next few moments of our conversation, I realized just how much had been said about me in circles of people that I was sure loved me. She paused and said,

"I want you to serve, but I don't want people to know that you're coming. If they know you're coming, that could cause them to change their minds."

For the life of me, I could not understand why my losses and my processes caused people to respond so offensively. Despite the hurt I felt, I agreed to serve, with hopes that the weekend would go much better than expected. A few weeks later, we met in their normal place, where we would catch up and confirm carpools, etc. I had my Husband drop me off early, because I wanted to have some time to prepare myself for whatever might happen. After I few moments, I began hearing a few familiar voices, one who was my mentor before I fell of the face of the earth. She had not seen me nor did she know I was there, so as I sat and waited all I could do was pray. She along with the whole team came walking around corner. I smiled and waved looking nervous and excited. Screams filled the room, as my mentor, among others rushed over to hug me. She sat right beside me as we caught up, laughed, and just took a moment to process. As we hit the road and headed up the mountain, I sat grateful at how God had completely shifted me and now here I sat, among some of the people I thought would never accept me, and for sure, would never have accepted me back.

We arrived and prepared for the first session which was specific to repentance. My mentor came over to me, sat down, looked at me and smiled. She then paused and said,

"I need to repent to you. I should have come and got you when you left."

I paused, smiled back, and said,

"It's totally okay. There are some places that only God can rescue us from."

This weekend became one of restoration, redemption, healing and more as I said yes to the call of deliverance ministry on my life. This one moment in time would turn into cycles and years of serving in this way, until life shifted, and the game of sorts, changed.

If I can be honest, I have always been one who loved bringing people together, so when the opportunity arose for me to bring powerful and purposed women together, I jumped at the chance. I did not know much about the organization's founders but felt that it was something that I could grow from and as a result, introduce other women to. By this time, I knew what it meant to feel support and likewise, what the lack of it felt like as well. It was with this in mind that I would oftentimes push everyone else's dream, yes, even more than my own and for this vision, it was no different. Within a year, God enabled me to lead, recruit and establish our North Carolina chapter, of almost eighty women strong, and shortly thereafter, our South Carolina chapter as well.

This effort landed me an award but in order to receive it, I would have to travel to Maryland. With our finances beyond tight, the trip seemed impossible, until my husband, knowing I wanted to be there, sold his car for scraps, just enough for gas and a hotel room to get us there and back home. We jumped in our Ford Explorer and took to the road. There was nothing like meeting my "sisters" for the very first time, along with receiving an award! My work didn't require one, I just wanted everyone to prosper, no more, no less.

Time flew and our anniversary was right around the corner. I knew that this would be the perfect time for the ladies to host a power-filled event on behalf of the state, as we invited all of the sisters from the other chapters. We spared no expense, even landing some of us to spend the last dime that we had. The ladies showed up in record numbers. That night, I shared the Word of God, as we opened up the conference. That night seemed to go smoothly, but the next day, not so much. The gathering concluded, and right when I thought I was approaching a conversation of amazing feedback, I was instead challenged with questions that completely threw me off. What was asked of me caused me to literally empty my pockets, though what I had was just enough to keep the lights on in our home.

Monday morning came, and a meeting was scheduled. I called defenses up as I had not only spent the time processing our exchange, but also had received word of how some of our ladies were treated. I came on the line ready to defend, make it right, and come to some resolve to move forward. Before I knew it, the line got heated as I heard her utter these words:

"If you don't agree with me, then you're not with us at all. If that's the case I need you to resign."

Stunned was an understatement, because after all, who else had been willing to sell whatever just to be where they were needed for a vision that wasn't even theirs? By the end of the conversation, she communicated with the ladies I served with to advise them that I had resigned (though I had not), and that anyone who wanted my position could have it. In addition, she communicated to most and suggested to some, that they completely disconnect from me. Just like that over one hundred, seventy-five women, some of who I had known for years, turned away from me, and completely disassociated themselves. This later escalated to the realm of hurt and pain as I spoke with some down the road who admitted that they let me go because, even though I had known them longer, she and the organization had more influence than me. The plot thickened as some even began removing me from fliers for events that had no ties to the organization, and even others who claimed connection to me, only to admit that they really just tolerated me until something happened to take me out. This served as the foundation of the refusal of words like "sis," because for me, it sounded and resembled a snake, one who just wanted squeeze me for all I had until there was nothing left.

While one would think that life would slow down there, it didn't. No sooner than two months down the road, our current Bishop released instructions to us to begin a bible study in the city of Greensboro. Immediately I kicked and screamed, knowing that to go from club girl would be a task within itself, but this time I wasn't submitting alone. I looked at my Husband who before I could even say no and justify why, shook his head yes, and consequently, so did I.

We were not given any members to begin with, as the instructions were that we had to build from the ground up. We promoted that we were beginning a bible study and prepared for our first night of teaching, September 6, 2012. I was still working in corporate America and, needless to say, they could have cared less about me following God's plan for my life. I remember that day, as I sat and contemplated what to do, as we were committed to beginning that day. My early request had been denied, and so this major decision sat before me, stay, or go. Now while some may ask why I had to choose, for me it was the only option I had — I had already been singled out as my body adjusted to pregnancy and landed me sick at my desk for many days.

For those who have ever worked in a call center, you know that these matters don't go over well, so at 5:25pm that day, with the blessing of my Husband, I shredded my work documents, cleaned my desk and left a letter of resignation for my supervisor, call center manager and human resources department. By 7:00pm there we sat, my family and I, waiting for people to just about knock the door over, but no one knocked, no one rang the doorbell, not one person at all.

That night, we reported back to our Bishop that there were four in attendance, my husband, our son, my daughter (who we were claiming was a girl at this time,) and myself. This faith move later turned into a bible study room full of people in our home, and would less than one year later, on January 27, 2013 become a church, where we would Pastor. A room filled with over two hundred people that day, turned into eight people in our living room, as we went from having a place to meet to having none at all. The word from the host church was this, that they were not used to a crowd showing up in numbers like that nor were they used to the move of God displayed and therefore, we were no longer permitted to use the space. Talk about blackballed.

It was with this news that we began the transformation of the first floor of our home, into our church. A sign that I created on our laser jet printer became the signage on the door held up by scotch tape. The wood floor entry of our home became the church foyer, and the couches became our seating. Our kitchen table held the position of the sacred desk as a floating desk corner shelf and Dollar Tree curtains covered the table. No sound system? No problem! A karaoke machine became our praise and worship station, our minister of music; what irony in light of how I began as a child.

For months, we operated this way, while using my prayer room right off the kitchen as the pastoral study. Two months after our opening, our daughter was born, and it was that moment I believed showed the people how serious we were about the call of God on our lives. Having almost died giving birth, and body bags being held waiting for my daughter and I to die, I only had one question, "How long will it take for me to go home? We have church on Sunday!" Needless to say, my daughter and I defied the odds, and two days after her birth were on our way home right in time for church!

Eventually there was no more room — people occupied every seat and even our staircase, too. By the end of the summer, we were "forced" to move into what would become our new home, Bain Street, where miracles, signs and wonders would take place. We expanded, we grew and even matured from the karaoke machine to a sound system, drums, a keyboard, pulpit, and podium made of zip ties and PVC pipe, crafted by my husband. We worshiped in that place. We experienced miracles there. Within two years, we went from being completely complacent to being challenged by the Lord, with a new direction and new name.

One would think that shifts like these would come well supported, but unfortunately, that was not the case. There we sat with a name before us, "Maximizing Life," a name that started out as a men's conference years before he even met me. He spoke the Word of the Lord, and knowing that it was time, we reached out to our covering to let them know how God was leading us. After conversations were attempted, we knew it was time and with all of the sincerity in our hearts, submitted a letter notifying them of our shift. Within what had to be a week's time, we received notification of receipt stating that as a result of our decision, everything sown into us for the start of ministry would be reclaimed and removed from our church — this included chairs, mics, sound systems, everything. All of this hit us like a ton of bricks as we prepared for the latest thing God had charged us to do, a prayer walk.

The day of the walk came, but not before 10:00am, as a white van met us at the church. Chairs were stacked and pushed to the door, along with speakers and everything else demanded based on the letter received. Along with the letter there were instructions that we were not allowed to preach until given permission, all at the hands of one I called father. I trusted him with my life, with my call, and now, there I stood before him, almost invisible, no eye contact at all, hurt all around for sure. Those who came with him tried their best to bandage the situation and even years later, would reach out to apologize, but I must say, it is one thing to bury your father, but another thing to lose the one you had grown to call father and be forced to treat him like the walking dead. Believe it or not, our prayer walk still happened hours later from this moment. I can say that it is only by the strength of God that we survived that day, as we walked through downtown Greensboro, with a prayer flag and oil in hand, over twenty people, black, white, Christian and even agnostic "believers."

That day people were healed, and you remember my friend from the club, Tasha, well that day, she gave her heart to the Lord; to this day, it still reigns as one of my greatest memories. Days and weeks were filled with tears and even attempts to make peace. Responses came as disconnected lines and technical phone failures; for us the disconnect became our disconnect as we trusted God to heal and carry us to the next place. I don't know if God sent a Holy APB out or what, but within days, everything that had been taken away had been replaced with better and more! A pastor who was coming to minister at our church, was awakened in the middle of an event we hosted at our church. As she described it, she was commissioned to help us recover and did just that. God used her to connect the dots, to replace and restore, right in time for the revival we had scheduled weeks before.

For us, we had never known anyone who had to recover from such a hit and had no idea that there would be more to come. Eventually, we were able to relocate to our next church location, not far from our first. It had been vacant for years, so of course we had some major cleaning up to do. It was through this process that I discovered that with move and vision, loss sometimes comes, as some who started with us decided that was the place where they got off. Whether it be because of the building, time or both, we reluctantly accepted what we had never been taught to survive.

11.

WHEN NO IS NO LONGER AN OPTION

The funny thing about YES, is that it doesn't care anything about your NO, and for us, this truth could not have become more clearer than the year of 2018. By then, we had taken more hits than a little bit, from church packed, to church splits. Hurt hit differently for me, because remember, I was leading in my hometown, and therefore being subject to losing not just church members, but even childhood and college friends, too. I released many things for the church, for my YES to God, especially friendships. Ministry continued; some days it felt like a dream and others, a nightmare. There were days we felt as if things were finally coming together only to find out it was really falling apart. Among the losses was one I considered to be my best friend. She was gorgeous, smart, and one for whom I have to give credit where credit is due, for she was my pusher when it came to publishing my first book.

I knew nothing about publishing, so to publish two books in less than a year was crazy, but a God-move to me! The day of my book signing, with my to-do list in hand, I texted her to see if she was coming. The reply nearly ripped my heart out,

"No, I'm not coming. I should let you know too, that I am not coming back to church either.

We won't be back."

The day of my book signing, I lost my best friend and a co-laborer all in the same breath. I looked up from my phone, with not a word to describe where I was, but only knowing that I had to push through that day, and push I did! The next day, Sunday came and I found myself standing before a now majority empty room, trying to sing past my hurt. Let me be clear, I did not want to sing, as being told to "shut up" because I "couldn't" caused me to quiet my sound. This word over me came on the heels of the preparation of being on a young man's album who I attended high school with. (Yes, you read it right, I carried the word to STOP singing from age sixteen until I was in my thirties.)

I stood before a room of folding chairs that Sunday, praying and hoping that she would walk around the corner at any moment with her kids, but that moment never came. As I sang, I crashed to the floor, but continued to push, as a glimmer of hope walked in, a member who had left with two visitors. Joy filled my heart as I just knew that she was there to come back, only to later find out that she came to gloat and show her friends what she had been self-professing with her chest out,

"See what I did to destroy their church?"

Hits came, but so did God's glory, even still and even the more and that truth was undeniable. One Sunday afternoon we pushed into a powerful yet heartbreaking service as we processed the loss of one our newest members, Shima, who was and to this day is, the dopest female drummer and one of my most prized mentees ever. We left church that day, with her family on our mind. By that afternoon, we were at her apartment helping her husband go through papers and try to make sense of her unexpected loss. As we worked, the wind blew, and at one point, it became alarming, but we kept working. Before we knew it, our phones began to go off with alerts of a tornado that had occurred in the neighborhood of our church. We received confirmation and then word, that the place where our church resided could not been seen as the roadway was covered by trees. The entire night, we were faced with not knowing what our church looked like or how we would even proceed.

The next day came, and we had two things on the agenda, saying our final goodbyes to Shima and seeing the remains of our church. After the hardest reality hit ever at the funeral home, we got in our car and rode up the street as close as we could get, to our church. It looked like a movie set, with cops, live wires, and debris everywhere. With our kids in tow and a few other members, we walked through the debris and finally made it to our church. As we approached, we could not believe what we saw, the two businesses that were attached completely destroyed, the house that was next to us, blown across the street and our church, seemingly untouched. We walked up and upon entry saw nothing unmoved, AT ALL. Our offices were still intact, even down to the greeting cards on our desks; there was no noticeable damage until we got to the youth room and finally, the sanctuary but nothing in comparison to the businesses that had been attached to us.

There I stood, and later sat on the grass, with no other response than to weep. As I lay with my face planted to the ground I heard footsteps.

"Hey! Is that doctor going to be in today?"

I looked up, then stood, then looked around as if to say, "lady do you not SEE THIS?"

She looked at me, as my face relayed the message.

"Hold up," she continued, "Ain't that a church right there."

"Yes ma'am," I replied with a face full of tears.

"I bet 'dey got some good stuff in there, huh? I wonder where the pastors are!?"

With shock in my eyes, I stood toe to toe with her and said, "right here."

She looked.

Her mouth could have hit the floor one million times.

Then, she turned, and ran away.

I immediately ran to my husband and told him what happened. His response was simple, "We've got to move out, TODAY."

For the rest of that day, we solicited boxes, secured the truck of one of our members and began tossing everything we could salvage on it. Everything moved so quickly that we didn't even think about eating.

Thank God for the same pastor who showed up to help us restore along with others who came to ensure that we ate, as they handed us food while they grabbed our boxes to continue packing. Despite the loss, believe it or not, we did not cancel church one time. The week after the loss of our building we secured our next place and held our first service there the following Sunday, the Pleasant Garden Fire House, followed by The Core Church in Greensboro, The YWCA and the Renaissance Event Center with a host of restaurants and not-so-ordinary places, before securing our new church home in March 2020.

Now that we have talked history, let's talk real — though our movements "looked" strong, we wanted to quit. I cannot tell you how many times we tried, only for our YES to laugh at us in the face. Every time we asked other leaders how to survive a tornado the ones that had an answer, who had never endured it had the same response,

"Close your church and just come over here. Bring your people. I know they put in work; we could use y'all over here."

If the conversation wasn't about us coming to them, it usually went a little something like this,

"I can't wait until y'all quit; I can get that catchy name y'all got. I can't believe God didn't give it to me first."

These pieces of "advice" became game changers for us, as we worked daily to pick up the pieces of a dream that many didn't understand. With a few people, two of whom had been there from day one and are still there (thank you EJ and E'Nique), we worked tirelessly to rebuild, retain, and recover from what most said was impossible. We said NO one million times, but God said YES one million times plus one. People found themselves following us even on social media having heard about our many trials and recovery processes, so much so that their "drive" became, "I'm just here to watch you bounce back." It was with this that we discovered that the bounce back had to become the COME UP, full recovery from all that we had lost, and redemption for all there was to gain, our RE-year.

12.

THE EMANCIPATION OF "B"

For my forty-third birthday, I asked my goddaughter, Dashona to make a design for me, a hoodie with the following on the back of it,

The Emancipation of B.

[1]Emancipation by definition means, "the social, or process of being set free from legal, social or political restrictions; liberation," and wholeheartedly, this was exactly what I needed. I was tired; I had reflected all of 2021, and by this point, had decided that a big part of me was done with people, places, destiny. I knew that some of what I had tolerated was an "inner me" issue, but I could not help but acknowledge the outside attacks, too. I looked and reflected as I remembered how much I had given of myself, to the point of exhaustion, and yes inner-hatred. Truth be told, I wanted out — the spirit of suicide hit me at fourteen years old, then again at eighteen, and in my twenties and thirties, and was now showing up in my forties. The more I wanted to let go, the more God

---

[1] www.google.com

reminded me of why I couldn't. It did not matter who left or even what they said when they did, God was holding on to me and though part of me had given up the ghost, God wouldn't accept it.

It was here that I realized that I just wanted to be free – absent of pain, and living the life that God ordained. It's amazing how one can look around and feel like no one else is going through what you are going through, all while God reveals conversations, revelations, secret affiliations and more. As life continued, I eventually had to come to grips with the truth, The mantle that I possessed traveled through generations, whether by family or mentors, so saying YES and gaining my freedom in HIM was the key.

36 So if the Son makes you free, then you are unquestionably free.

John 8:36

For years, I had lived wrapped up in the cocoon and, I would even say tomb, of others' opinions and permissions, too. I had grown weary of being looked at like a charity case, as people who had heard our story approached with puppy dog eyes lacking compassion. I became bitter with my call, as I asked God the infamous question that many of us were warned never to ask,

"Why?"

It was here that I came to understand that this three-letter forbidden word does not offend God, but instead, expresses a human void fit for His impartation. Why became my go to word, not as a spoiled response, but merely as a child unto the Father needing clarity for my life. Emancipation for me though, included the acceptance of never knowing why.

Why did You take my father?

Why did You give me a mantle from a man, my grandfather, who I never even knew?

Why didn't You just let me die when I wanted to?

Why did you allow my whole life to be altered in seemingly one hit?

Why didn't You punish those church people for abandoning me?

Why did You let all of my mentors die?

Why did You allow us to be embarrassed as a church so many times?

Why do I have to be coined as "the black sheep?"

Why am I always underestimated?

I knew, had I asked a man that question, offense would have been their response, but as I asked God, some questions had answers while some had silence which equated to peace. For every question that had no answer, God brought someone with the very same request. My question still pended as God used me to answer the requests of His people. I answered, and in those very moments, God answered me.

"Because I am God. Even when you don't get it, I'm God. Don't you see, for every situation you have named, I have proven to be your answer? Losing your father so soon wasn't fair, but have I not proven to be Father to you? Suicide wanted to have you, but have you forgotten that I control the hand of death? When you felt alone, was my accomplishments through you not enough and when you felt like a black sheep, it was only my anointing and setting you apart. You said it yourself, there are simply some places that man would NEVER come to get you, but I came, I showed up, to rescue you, right in the nick of time. So, Brandi, Daughter, stop it. I've always been here, and I always will be, right here, with you."

For years I asked God to emancipate me, and in one fleeting moment, He did just that. As I look around this space at 2:48am EST, I do so knowing that God has kept me through it all.

When I didn't know if my son and I would make it, we did.

When I wasn't sure if God could give me the marriage He showed me, He did.

When I didn't know if I could ever forgive my past to embrace my present and future, He did.

When I didn't think that God would ever forgive me for committing the unimaginable, He did, and even entrusted me with more, natural children, godchildren, and spiritual children, too.

God, my Father, my Daddy, The Great Emancipator.

[5] For I,' declares the LORD, 'will be a wall of fire around her [protecting her from enemies], and I will be the glory in her midst.'"

Zechariah 2:5

Brandi L. Rojas

Wife I Mother I Pastor I Entrepreneur I Visionary I Mentor

Pastor Brandi L. Rojas is a native of Greensboro, N.C. She serves with her Husband, Pastor Omar Rojas at Maximizing Life Family Worship Center in Greensboro, N.C. a vision God birthed through them in 2015. Rojas has been in Dance Ministry for over 20 years and is a 2009 graduate of the School of Disciples taught under the late Bishop Otis Lockett, Sr.; in 2013, she was named Sweetheart of the Triad, an award given based on community involvement. Pastor Rojas was licensed to preach the Gospel on February 27, 2011, and as a result DYmondFYre Global Ministries was born. Rojas was ordained as an Elder June 22, 2012, and was installed as Pastor with her Husband on January 27, 2013.

Since that time, she and her Husband, also known as #TeamRojas, by God's mandate, have birthed several evangelistic causes. In January 2014 Rojas opened FYreDance Studios which provides on-site instruction, virtual teaching, consultation services, choreography services and dance encounters. The following year, in 2015, a prayer walk initiative was created to bring the local churches and community together to work together and help lead the lost to Jesus Christ and empower the world through a vehicle called The Gatekeeper's Legacy; since that time she has also served as part of the planning and leadership committee for the National Day of Prayer for the City of Greensboro and currently serves as the youngest committee member, only African-American and only female on the core team.

In February 2016, Rojas launched out again to begin IgniteHerSoul International Women's Fellowship (formerly The Legacy Ladies Fellowship), an organization created to help women of God pray, push, and live the reality of what God has called them to. The CrossOver Resource Center was later birthed out of the mandate of Maximizing Life FWC, which works to provide solutions for life's transitions to the community. Rojas released her first book in June 2016 entitled **In the Face of Expected Failure** and her sophomore project, **Humpty Dumpty in Stilettos: The Great Exchange**, in November 2016. It was with the second book release Fiery Beacon Publishing House, LLC was launched, serving current and upcoming authors, playwrights, and poets. Since that time, she along with her FBPH Team have been able to help over 115 authors launch and pursue their literary dreams along with owning the first noted Author Incubator Hub, "The

Ink Lab," offered by a publishing house, giving literary creatives a safe place to think and CREATE. Fiery Beacon Publishing House, LLC also holds an A+ rating with the Better Business Bureau and currently reigns as the only publishing house to do so within their region and beyond. **Humpty Dumpty in Stilettos** was nominated for the National Literary Trailblazer of the Year Award in 2017 by the Indie Author Legacy Award in Baltimore, Maryland and in July 2017 she was noted as an International Best-Selling Author for her part in a collaborative effort called **Stories from the Pink Pulpit: Women in Ministry Speak.** She has since then been recognized as a multiple best-selling author for her involvement in various projects and releases.

Rojas has added to her list a number of other literary works including: **Rehobeth Church Road: Suicide in the Pulpit** (September 2019), her first publishing company collaboration, **When Legacy Arises from the Threshing Floor: A Collective of Trials and Tribulations Superseded by Undeniable Triumphs** (November 2019), **Before You Hit 40: Forty-One Pivotal Life Nuggets** (January 2020), **Not With Your Legs Crossed: #SpiritualBirthingUncensored** (September 2020), **My Pink Stilettos** (October 2020), **When Legacy Arises from the Threshing Floor: A Collective of Trials and Tribulations Superseded by Undeniable Triumphs Volume 2** (November 2020), **The Mantle I Never**

Asked For (November 2020), **Not With Your Legs Crossed #SpiritualBirthingUncensored, and Church Girl, Club Girl, God's Girl** with additional releases coming soon!

In the Marketplace, beyond Fiery Beacon Publishing House, LLC, Pastor Rojas is known for her progressive efforts through her travel company, Fiery Beacon Travel, and the international platform of Surge365. She currently serves as a Regional Builder with the company, has been called on by top executives to share presentations, team building encouragement and more, and has received multiple bonuses while doing so. Rojas also makes it a priority to share the reality and necessity of multiple streams of income which empowers the home, community, nation, and world. Pastor Rojas is grateful and humbled at how God continues to expand the entire vision, not just to the United States, but internationally as well.

To add to her list of God-given accomplishments and mandates, Rojas stepped into the world of music in January 2023 with the release of her debut EP, "The FYre Room: Volume 1," a collective of prophetic sounds and declarations for the nations. It was by way of this project that she also tried her hand as a song writer and succeeded.

Team Rojas are the proud parents of five children, and three godchildren. Pastor Brandi Rojas is a Worshiper, Servant,

Praise Vessel, and Prayer Warrior, but most of all, she is a vessel who is on fire for God.

Connect with Author Brandi Rojas

Email:

fbphinfo@fierybeaconpublishinghousellc.com

Facebook:

https://www.facebook.com/FieryBeaconPHLLC

Instagram:

@allthingsdymondfyre

Made in the USA
Columbia, SC
25 February 2025

54428086R00098